# Abide

Putting Down Roots into the Word of Life

James C. Wilhoit

kindle direct publishing

Available through Amazon

With appreciation to

John Kleinig

Who taught me much about Bible

meditation through his writings

# Contents

# Preface

I began this writing project, like so many others, with a question. I wanted to understand what the Bible meant by meditation and to discover what this practice actually involves. As I read and studied, I found people and sources that helped guide what was initially an academic project and soon became very personal and life-giving. I found myself drawn into practicing the meditation patterns I was finding in the Bible and began setting aside an hour each day to meditate on the Bible. Authors often find that they unwittingly write the books they need to read, and this volume is no exception. I needed to deepen and renew my meditation practice, and I have recorded what I learned on this journey of discovery.

I have learned and experienced much through this eighteen-month project. Since my earliest days as a newly committed Christian, now fifty-five years ago, I have known about the call in Scripture to meditate on Scripture. I have long had a practice of daily Bible reading, which included meditation. The careful study of what Scripture says about meditation has brought about a renewal in my own practice.

Three insights that came early in my study have deeply affected what it now means for me to meditate. The first was realizing that while we take for granted that Psalm 1 speaks of the person who meditates, the first English translations did not use the word meditate. The first complete English translation by Myles Coverdale rendered Psalm 1 as the blessed person "exercises himself in his law." That term caught my imagination. Unwittingly I had come to think of meditation as a somewhat passive activity, and the realization that it is more akin to doing a tough math exercise than daydreaming or introspection. Second, I am grateful for the Puritans and their emphasis on meditation, I realized I had made the Puritans' portrayal the gold standard of meditation. Yet, what they describe could only happen with readily available printed Bibles, in homes with desks and lighting and with easy access to pens and paper. What they suggest is good and helpful for their time and place, but the Puritan method of meditation would not have been feasible in ancient Israel. The Old Testament call to meditate was first given to nomadic people, most of whom were illiterate and did not have access to printed Bibles. The practice of meditation in the Bible was to be done throughout the day on texts that had been memorized, on truths that had been internalized, and during the divine service when Scripture was read. I was also helped by John Kleinig's thoughtful portrayal of Jesus as the Master Meditator. Taking time to see how our Lord was a meditator gave me a renewed commitment to the calling to meditate.

Despite having taught courses in Christian spirituality for decades and having a rich personal prayer life, I remain a materialist. Things and political events are the first to get my attention. I will say that this eighteen-month engagement with Bible meditation has done much to lessen the pull of the material world. I have long prayed a prayer by John Ballie as an aspiration that the pull of the world would lessen and I believe through a renewed emphasis on meditation, it has. Here is a portion of his prayer.

Do not let me go into my work believing only in the world of sense and time, but give me grace to understand that the world I cannot see or touch is the most real world of all. My life today will be lived in time, but it will involve eternal issues. The needs of my body will shout out, but it is for the needs of my soul that I must care the most. My business will be with material things, but let me be aware of spiritual things behind them. Let me always keep in mind that the things that matter are not money or possessions, not houses or property, not bodily comforts or pleasures, but truth and honor and gentleness and helpfulness and a pure love of you. John Ballie

There are a number of people who made this project possible. I had the joy of finding an intellectual mentor in my study. Early in my literature review, I came across the work of John Kleinig, an Australian Old Testament professor whose careful work and theological grounding for meditation proved so helpful. He answered my emails and pointed me to various valuable sources.

The library staff at Buswell Library provided invaluable support as they helped me track down hard to find articles and books, which proved to be so helpful in this study. In the spring of 2014, I spent a semester at the Center for Christian Thought at Biola University, funded through a generous grant from the Templeton Foundation, and it was there that the seeds were sown for this current project. I also did some initial study on this subject while in residence at Tyndale House in Cambridge, UK. Klaus Issler and Evan Howard read the manuscript and provided helpful feedback. And I am grateful for my dear wife Carol on many accounts, and in this context, especially grateful for her careful and thoughtful reading of the manuscript at various times.

# – 1 –

# The Way of Flourishing

Blessed Lord, who caused all holy Scriptures to be written for our learning: Grant us so to hear them, read, mark, learn, and inwardly digest them, that we may embrace and ever hold fast the blessed hope of everlasting life, which you have given us in our Savior Jesus Christ; who lives and reigns with you and the Holy Spirit, one God, for ever and ever. Amen.

Book of Common Prayer

## Being Deeply Rooted

This book is about putting down roots so you can flourish as God intended. You'll learn to heed the call to let your roots sink deep into Scripture so that "your roots will grow down into God's love and keep you strong" (Eph. 3:17 NLT).

Marilynne Robinson's *Gilead* tells the story of a faithful pastor in rural Iowa. Near the end of the book, this reflective pastor, John Ames, exclaims, "I love the prairie! So often I have seen the dawn come and the light flood over the land and everything turn radiant at once, that word 'good' so profoundly affirmed in my soul that I am amazed I should be

Now there is in the Holy Scriptures a book which is distinguished from all other books of the Bible by the fact that it contains only prayers. The book is the Psalms. It is at first very surprising that there is a prayer book in the Bible...This is pure grace, that God tells us how we can speak with him and have fellowship with him. We can do it by praying in the name of Jesus Christ. The Psalms are given to us to this end, that we may learn to pray them in the name of Jesus Christ.

Dietrich Bonhoeffer

allowed to witness such a thing." I, too, have grown to love the prairie. It is a very different beauty from the forests of my boyhood home in Oregon, but a place where I see, as John Ames did, "the good." Tallgrass prairies are a highly complex web of life and far more diverse than I initially understood. In the late summer, I especially love my prairie walks and bike rides, when the tallgrass is complemented by some of my favorite showy plants, like compass plants, goldenrod, milkweed, and asters. At this time of year, some grasses are taller than I am. Yet I only notice a fraction of the prairie, because three-quarters of the prairie's biomass, its plant material, is underground. Prairies thrive because they are deeply rooted.

Prairies are amazingly resilient. The prairie I visit most often is burned every spring to control invasive plants so that desirable native species with deep root systems can thrive. I watch it emerge each spring and return to its summer glory. My familiar prairie reminds me of the call to put our roots down deep, to give attention to what is out of sight. Prairies are stunning, in part, because they are not just all show. They are not like cut flowers, which are beautiful for a day or two and then are ready to be tossed aside. Instead, their deep and extensive roots allow them to flourish through drought and other harsh conditions.

## Blessed and Deeply Rooted

The Book of Psalms is the most unusual book in the Bible. A testimony to its uniqueness is that it often is printed as a single book. Images, not stories or arguments, convey the message of this book, and those images connect deeply with our emotions and experiences. Word precision and structured phrases

# Psalm 1

[1] Happy is the one
> who does not walk in the counsel of the
> wicked,
> and does not stand in the way of the sinners,
> and does not sit in the seat of scoffers.

[2] Rather, whose delight is in the instruction of the LORD,
> who meditates on his instruction day and
> night.

[3] This one is like a tree transplanted by streams of water,
> which produces its fruit in its season,
> Whose leaves do not wither;
> but who prospers in everything.

[4] Not so the wicked!
> Rather, they are like chaff that the wind drives away.
[5] Therefore the wicked will not arise in the judgment,
> nor sinners in the assembly of the righteous.
[6] For the LORD knows the way of the righteous,
> but the way of the wicked will perish.

abound, and the images often communicate their message by placing objects side by side in comparison. It is the book quoted most often in the New Testament, and it is the one Jesus quoted the most. The psalms were the songs he sang, and they tell about him. As Christians, we understand that psalms point to Jesus and our life with God. It is a book of prayers, to be sure, and meditation is an important theme throughout it as well. The two opening psalms have been called meditations on meditation.

Psalm 1 was placed at the beginning to serve as an introduction to this collection of poems. Psalm 1 invites us to meditate on the psalms that follow. This psalm gives us a picture of the good person, someone who is flourishing. While the only person who has fully lived the life pictured in this psalm is Jesus, the psalm invites us to adopt the pattern of living and the success that it pictures. When we consider the promised flourishing of the psalms, it is worth remembering this is not a promise of an easy life. Jesus, our model meditator, flourished in his life and ministry, but he did not have an easy life. This psalm reminds the reader that meditation is the God-given pathway to enjoying a deeply satisfying life. When happiness is mentioned in the psalms, it means more than an abundance of pleasure. John Wesley, in a sermon on love, captures the classic Christian understanding of what is meant by real happiness: "By happiness I mean, not a slight, trifling pleasure, that perhaps begins and ends in the same hour; but such a state of well-being as contents the soul, and gives it a steady, lasting satisfaction."

The Psalms are the prayer
book of the Bible, but it is
noteworthy that the first
Psalm is not a prayer per se
but a meditation—in fact, it is
a meditation on meditation.

Tim Keller

At the outset of this psalm, we are told that the blessed person avoids harmful entanglements and instead delights in and meditates on the Law of God. Meditation and delight in Scripture go hand in hand. Consider these statements in the psalms:

- "Whose delight is in the law of the LORD, and who meditates on his law day and night" (Ps. 1:2 NIV).
- "I meditate on your precepts . . . I delight in your decrees" (Ps. 119:15–16 NIV).
- "I reach out for your commands, which I love, that I may meditate on your decrees" (Ps. 119:48 NIV).
- "Oh, how I love your law! I meditate on it all day long" (Ps. 119:97 NIV).

Meditation is delight-fueled thinking. *The Bay Psalm Book* (1640), the first book published in British North America, nicely captures this emphasis with the phrase, "But in the law . . . is his longing delight." There is a strong connection between what delights us and what captures the focus of our meditation. As you consider developing your practice of meditating on the Bible, coming to appreciate and delight in the Bible is the pathway to meditation. One of the lessons I have learned in life is that meditation happens. I will meditate, in the sense of brooding on and worrying about or obsessing over, what I care about. Meditation, dwelling on what we value, is part of the human experience. The call is to transform our thinking so that we dwell on God. And one pathway to do that is not simply by trying to do this but by training our minds through deliberate meditation.

The connection between delight and meditation is

It is a good thing to let prayer be the first business of the morning and the last at night.

Martin Luther

pictured in Psalm 2:1. Here, the enemies of God and his rightful King are portrayed as being in conflict. The question is posed, "Why do the nations conspire and the peoples plot in vain?" (NIV). The word translated "plot" is the same word rendered as "meditate" in Psalm 1:2. In one case, delight in the Law prompts a person to focus and daydream about the beauty of God's order, and in the other case, the hatred of God's King drives his enemies to murmur and conspire to attack him. These two psalms are a gateway to the Psalter. In Psalm 1, meditation on God's Law leads to a person being a deeply planted and fruitful tree. In Psalm 2, nations, peoples, kings, and officials murmur against the Lord and his anointed king, and this leads to the nations being dashed "to pieces like pottery" (Ps. 2:9 NIV). I must underscore that the "happy way" of Psalm 1 is not easy or always pleasant, but it is the way of well-being and deep fulfillment.

## The Power of Bible Engagement

Lifeway Research conducted a large multi-year research study on spiritual well-being. This study confirmed the church's well-established pastoral wisdom: Bible engagement changes lives. They found that "Bible engagement," a broad category that captures activities such as reading, hearing, studying, or meditating on the Bible, is one of the eight key attributes of discipleship. Ed Stetzer, the research director, said, "Bible engagement has an impact in just about every area of spiritual growth." Another comprehensive study of spiritual growth had a similar finding. "Best-practice churches make Bible engagement practical, meaningful, and accessible"; they all "share a focused and firm commitment to get

Without meditation the truths which we know will never affect our hearts...As a hammer drives a nail to the head, so meditation drives a truth to the heart... Read before you meditate. "Give attendance to readings" (1 Tim. 4:13). Then it follows, "meditate upon these things" (vs. 15). Reading doth furnish with matter; it is the oil that feeds the lamp of meditation. Be sure your meditations are founded upon Scripture. Reading without meditation is unfruitful; meditation without reading is dangerous.

Thomas Watson

their people to engage with the Bible in an ongoing fashion." In other words, this is not rocket science; engaging with Scripture in the presence of God promotes deep and lasting spiritual transformation.

Bible engagement may seem like an outdated and banal practice when compared with the allurement of media and ever-present electronic distractions. However, engaging the Bible is a time-tested spiritual activity. We all need to center down and experience guidance and comfort in God's Word. I do have a concern about the way the concept of Bible engagement is often discussed. These discussions can give the sense that all forms of Bible engagement are of equal value; moreover, Bible engagement is rarely clearly defined. Recently, someone mentioned that they were "not getting anything out of the Bible." When I asked about their reading practice, they said, "Oh, I listen to it on my phone while I do chores." It is safe to say that type of "Bible engagement" goes in one ear and out the other. The Bible is a holy book, not magical. It becomes a means of growth when we connect with it deeply. Consider this statement about the effects of Bible reading: "Blessed is the one who reads aloud the words of this prophecy, and blessed are those who hear it and take to heart what is written in it, because the time is near" (Rev. 1:3 NIV). Here we again see a connection between the well-lived life and rightly responding to God's Word. In this verse, the Greek word for "blessed" is the same word used to translate "happy" in Psalm 1. The Bible engagement portrayed in Revelation is rich. It involves oral reading, active listening, taking to heart (meditating), and rightly acting on the Word that has been meditated on, read,

What each man worships in preference to the rest, what he admires and loves above other things, this is God to him.

Origen

and heard. The Bible engagement that counts is the engagement that takes the Word into one's heart and leads to obedience.

# – 2 –

# True Spiritual Food

The light burns long in his study. He does
not always remain bent over the pages;
he often leans back, closes his eyes over
a line he has read again, and its sense
diffuses into his blood.

Rainer Maria Rilke

"You are what you eat." This truism captures the
thought that our health and vitality are affected by
what we consume. This message has been driven home
by countless studies showing how food consumption
patterns affect our health. What is true of our bodies
is also true for our spirits. In the great story of God's
redeeming love, eating "the forbidden fruit" changed
everything.

In the Garden of Eden, God chose to use a fruit
tree as a symbol of the knowledge of good and evil;
the act of eating that fruit constituted Adam and
Eve's disobedience (Gen. 2:17). The way God designed
humans to take food into their bodies so that it
becomes part of them paints the picture of the way
we open ourselves up to good or evil, taking in either
one or the other so that it becomes part of us. We can
eat spiritual food that gives life: "Take and eat; this
is my body" (Matt. 26:26 NIV). Or we can consume

Meditate on these things;
give yourself entirely to
them, that your progress
may be evident to all.

1 Tim. 4:15 NKJV

spiritual food that brings death. Isaiah describes the idol worshiper who "feeds on ashes" (Isa. 44:20 NIV) and dies spiritually. Idolaters consume ashes even though they believe they are feasting on spiritually nourishing food. Because ashes were often the result of battles, they are an image in the Bible of destruction, desolation, and waste. The irony is that while they dine on ashes, God would have it otherwise: "But you would be fed with the finest of wheat; with honey from the rock I would satisfy you" (Ps. 81:16 NIV). We are not to simply take note of God's spiritual food but to eat it, digest it, and allow it to nourish us.

The Bible portrays humans as spiritually hungry, thirsty, and on the prowl to satisfy this persistent desire. Augustine (AD 354–430) tells in his Confessions how his spiritual thirst drove him to a life of sensuality and status-seeking, memorably captured on the opening page: "In yourself, you rouse us . . . because you made us with yourself as our goal, and our heart is restless until it rests in you." Restless hearts only find deeply satisfying rest in God. And resting in God is the proper goal of life; "For Augustine, the goal of life is knowing and enjoying God."

The story told through the pages of the Bible is of God's relentless love and how people seek to satisfy their God-given thirst in other ways (through power, idolatry, pleasure, and money). The Bible openly acknowledges our thirst and unsettledness and invites everyone:

> Come, all you who are thirsty, come to the waters; and you who have no money, come, buy and eat! Come, buy wine and milk without money and without cost. Why spend money on what is not bread,

17

If I have time and opportunity to go through the Lord's Prayer, I do the same with the Ten Commandments. I take one part after another and free myself as much as possible from distractions in order to pray. I divide each commandment into four parts, thereby fashioning a garland of four entwined strands. That is, I think of each commandment as, first, instruction, which is really what it is intended to be, and consider what the Lord God so earnestly demands of me. Second, I turn it into a thanksgiving; third, a confession; and fourth, a prayer.

Martin Luther

and your labor on what does not satisfy?
Listen, listen to me, and eat what is good,
and your soul will delight in the richest of
fare (Isa. 55:1–2 NIV).

The invitation is clear. God invites us four times to "come." The invitation is extended to "all" who thirst, meaning everyone. It acknowledges our needs and gently warns us of the foolishness of buying bread that does not satisfy us.

One time when his disciples had returned from a trip into town to get food, they urged Jesus to eat something; Jesus told them he had food to eat that they knew nothing about (John 4:32). His answer confused them, and Jesus explained, "My food . . . is to do the will of him who sent me and to finish his work" (John 4:34 NIV). Seeking God and his kingdom was his food; it was what he thirsted and hungered for. It filled him and nourished him. Feasting on God enabled him to feed others: "I am the bread of life. Whoever comes to me will never go hungry, and whoever believes in me will never be thirsty" (John 6:35 NIV). Jesus is manna from heaven, the bread of life, the food that will satisfy our souls and give eternal life. He is the Word proceeding from the mouth of God by which men and women live (see Deut. 8:3; Isa. 55). When we feast on the Word, we draw sustenance from Christ; hence, biblical meditation is done with an awareness of God's presence with us.

When we feast on the Word, we do so with gusto, like Jeremiah when he wrote, "When your words came, I ate them; they were my joy and my heart's delight, for I bear your name, LORD God Almighty" (Jer. 15:16 NIV). Ezekiel, another prophet of this era, heard God telling him to take to heart his message

Why do I meditate? Because I am a Christian. Therefore, everyday in which I do not penetrate more deeply into the knowledge of God's Word in Holy Scripture is a lost day for me.

Dietrich Bonhoeffer

and internalize his teaching. He wrote, "As I opened my mouth, he gave me the scroll to eat, saying, 'Son of man, eat this book that I am giving you. Make a full meal of it!' So I ate it. It tasted so good—just like honey" (Ezek. 3:2–3 MSG). Through spiritual feasting on the Word of God, we receive the spiritual food that will satisfy us and allow us to grow in grace. Jesus is not only our bread but also our living water, welling up like a spring inside his disciples (John 4:14, 7:37–38).

This book tells about one way that we can eat and digest the spiritual food God has for us. One way to feast at God's rich banquet is by meditating on Scripture. We'll look more at what we mean by meditation and see what sets biblical meditation apart from all other forms of meditation. We are not just calming our minds or focusing on helpful affirmations; we are enjoying the company of Jesus. Like Mary, "who sat at the Lord's feet listening to what he said" (Luke 10:39 NIV), we listen to the voice of God, in God's presence, through Scripture, to hear and obey and to experience God's caress.

Another set of images for deep engagement with the Bible is that of putting down roots. We saw this image in Psalm 1, where the one who meditates "is like a tree transplanted by streams of water, which produces its fruit in its season." The life of the person who meditates on God's Law is compared to a deeply rooted tree. Meditators find sustaining nourishment in the life-giving soil of the riverbank. The tree was "transplanted," reminding us that meditation is not a self-improvement project but a God-ordained means of grace. We are being transplanted by grace to a soil that will sustain us. The roots anchor the tree in

Meditation, then, is what gives you stability, peace, and courage in times of great difficulty, adversity, and upheaval. It helps you stay rooted in divine "water" when all other sources of moisture—of joy, hope, and strength—dry up.

Tim Keller

place—anyone who has sought to move a shrub of any size knows how well roots accomplish this.

In his parable of the soils, Jesus gave us a warning as to what happens to a rootless plant:

> A farmer went out to plant some seeds. As he scattered them across his field, some seeds fell on a footpath, and the birds came and ate them. Other seeds fell on shallow soil with underlying rock. The seeds sprouted quickly because the soil was shallow. But the plants soon wilted under the hot sun, and since they didn't have deep roots, they died. Other seeds fell among thorns that grew up and choked out the tender plants. Still other seeds fell on fertile soil, and they produced a crop that was thirty, sixty, and even a hundred times as much as had been planted! (Matt. 13:3b–8 NLT)

Without roots going deep into the soil, the plant cannot thrive.

Jesus explained the parable's meaning: the seed represents the Word of God, and the story illustrates the importance of hearing well and rightly receiving the Word. In Luke's account, Jesus emphasized the importance of sustained retention of the Word. Those persons represented by the good soil "retain it" (Luke 8:15 NIV): they take it into their hearts and cling to it. They do this patiently and with careful attentiveness, producing "a huge harvest" (Luke 8:15 NLT). Attentive dwelling on the Word, where our roots sink into it deeply, results in fruitfulness.

What is out of sight, the root, is connected to what

My son, live according to what I am telling you; guard my instructions as you would a treasure deep within you...Bind cords around your fingers to remind you of them; meditate on them, and you'll engrave them upon your heart.

Prov. 7:1, 3 The Voice

sustains life. The remainder is simple—tend to your roots. Let them go deep into that which will nourish your soul, the riverbank of the Word of God, which keeps us "rooted and built up in him" (Col. 2:7 NIV). Our roots go down and draw our sustenance from him.

# – 3 –

# What Is Meditation?

These are only a few suggestions for committing yourself to the Word of God: Wait in silence before the Word. Read contemplatively. Be faithful to the reading whether you are moved by it or not. Listen obediently to the text. Discern how the Word is calling you to greater obedience. Pray as the Holy Spirit leads you. And finally, ABIDE. You are being invited to enter into an abiding presence with the Word of God.

Macrina Wiederkehr

Meditation is a broad and imprecise term in our culture. A health club offers a meditation class that focuses on self-calming techniques. Someone recovering from a bad accident learns meditation at a clinic to help deal with persistent pain. A Buddhist friend tells you about his lifelong meditation practice. Then your pastor preaches a sermon on biblical meditation and says that meditation is an essential Christian practice. Meditation can be a confusing catch-all term. Such confusion has not always marked the word meditation. The *Oxford English Dictionary* lists the first published use of meditate in English as being

The word meditate as used in the Old Testament literally means to murmur or to mutter and, by implication, to talk to oneself. When we meditate on the Scriptures, we talk to ourselves about them, turning over in our minds the meanings, the implications, and the applications to our own lives.

Though we use Psalm 119:11 in connection with Scripture memorization, it may be more supportive of the practice of meditation. The psalmist says God's Word was stored up in his heart—his inmost being. Bare memorization gets the Scriptures into only our minds. Meditation on those same Scriptures opens our understanding, engages our affections, and addresses our wills. This is the process of storing up the Word in our hearts.

Jerry Bridges

in Psalm 1:2 in the Geneva Bible (1560): "In his Law doeth he meditate day and night." The word meditate is widely used today, but notice that it was coined to describe a specific Christian spiritual practice. Initially, meditate referred to the Christian practice of prayerful contemplation of the Scriptures and was not applied to the wide range of activities that it is used for today.

When the Bible was first translated into English, the translators did not use the term meditate where you find it today. Instead, they used words that convey grappling with the text. For example, Psalm 1:2 today reads, "whose delight is in the law of the LORD, and who meditates on his law day and night" (NIV). However, in the first complete translation of the Bible in English by Myles Coverdale (1535), we find, "But delighteth in the law of the LORD, and exerciseth himself in his law both day and night" [spelling modernized]. In choosing the word exercise, Coverdale captured that the Hebrew word conveys a sense of active engagement with the text. In the *Oxford English Dictionary*, exercise (in Coverdale's time) conveyed the idea of "to employ, bring to bear...apply skill and make practical use of." We can think of a student doing math exercises or an athlete doing physical exercise. The emphasis is on active involvement and interaction with the Bible.

The biblical writers use a half dozen words for the multifaceted meditation process. In the original languages of the Bible, Greek and Hebrew, there was no technical term for the practice of meditation. "They used many terms to describe different aspects of the one process." The original words have primary meanings like "mutter," "speak," "sing," "think," "ponder," and "remember." Meditation has become

# Definitions of Meditation

Meditation is delight-driven pondering of Scripture with a receptive heart in the presence of Christ to foster our love of God and others.

James C. Wilhoit

Meditation then is the deliberate appropriation and retention of God's Word into the heart, so that the whole person is slowly transformed by it and begins to bear its fruit in his behaviour.

John Kleinig

Like all spiritual disciplines, Scripture meditation is another way to become more attentive to the still, small voice of God and to become more willing to respond when we hear it.

Jan Johnson

Meditation is the activity of calling to mind, and thinking over, and dwelling on, and applying to oneself, the various things that one knows about the works and ways and purposes and promises of God... It is an activity of holy thought, consciously performed in the presence of God, under the eye of God, by the help of God, as a means of communion with God.

J. I. Packer

Christian meditation, very simply, is the ability to hear God's voice and obey his word.

Richard Foster

...let's define meditation as deep thinking on the truths and spiritual realities revealed in scripture, or upon life from a scriptural perspective, for the purposes of understanding, application, and prayer. Meditation goes beyond hearing, reading, studying, and even memorizing as a means of taking in God's Word.

Don Whitney

the term most often used to describe a slow, thoughtful engagement with Scripture as the Word of God, but if you're not comfortable with the term meditation, consider something like "Bible intake," "Bible engagement," "abiding in the Word," "dwelling in Scripture," or "soaking in the Word." Do not let the term meditation trip you up.

## What Is Biblical Meditation?

In our English Bibles, you'll find two dozen references to meditation, almost all of which occur in the Psalms, a poetic book filled with images and focused on the praise of God. That points to meditation not being so much about informing us as about forming us as our hearts are stirred. Meditation is not portrayed as a technical skill to be mastered but as an outflow of our delight in his Word and a desire to love and obey him.

What does the Bible says about meditation?

There is minimal emphasis on how to meditate in the Bible. The focus is on the goal of dwelling on God's Word in his presence. Instead of looking for "the right way" to meditate, we should be focused on developing a habit of engaging with Scripture in God's presence.

The printed Bibles we take for granted have only been available for the past four hundred years. Jesus, our Master Meditator, meditated using memorized Scripture he had learned, probably in synagogue worship or at home. We, too, do well to memorize Scripture. When we do so, Scripture is always at hand for us to use for meditation. The meditation practices described in the Bible were done without easy access to written Bibles.

Pray over your meditations. Prayer fastens meditation upon the soul; prayer is a-tying a knot at the end of meditation that it doth not slip.

Thomas Watson

The primary focus of Christian meditation is Christ and his Word, truth, and God's creation. The breadth of what we should meditate on is captured by Paul: "Whatever is true, whatever is noble, whatever is right, whatever is pure, whatever is lovely, whatever is admirable—if anything is excellent or praiseworthy—think about such things" (Phil. 4:8 NIV).

Meditation involves our heart, which in the Bible is the seat of the emotions and the center of the "whole mind with all its faculties, such as thought, desire, emotion, and imagination." We need to enter into meditation with open hearts and train ourselves to see the images of the psalms and the details of a story with our mind's eye, so that our hearts are moved and healed as we dwell with Christ through his Word.

Meditation is a way to "humbly accept the word God has planted in your hearts" (James 1:21 NLT), and we should come with a relaxed openness and curiosity as we meditate.

Several words translated meditate describe embodied actions like muttering, singing, or speaking to oneself. In keeping with this physical emphasis in biblical meditation, embody your meditation practice: write, read aloud, draw, dance, or sing.

In secular meditation, the emphasis is often on the technique and meditation skills. In Christian meditation, the emphasis is different. We meditate in the presence of Christ and focus on his Word. Kleinig captures this emphasis well: "The decisive thing is not how we meditate, but on what we meditate."

David described coming to God after he had "calmed and quieted [himself]" (Ps. 131:2 NIV). Practices of walking or watching one's breath can

On some days, stand as a pilgrim before the Word of God. Visualize your movement down the path of words as a pilgrimage. The places where you choose to stop for further reflection are your pilgrim sites, your holy places along the way.

Macrina Wiederkehr

help one become still before God.

Two sides to biblical meditation are evident in Psalm 1 and throughout the writings of Paul. Notice how the blessed person of Psalm 1 avoids certain thought patterns. The righteous person, "does not walk in step with the wicked or stand in the way that sinners take or sit in the company of mockers." Instead, this one "meditates on his law" (Ps. 1:1–2 NIV). Likewise, Paul uses the language of changing clothes and urges his readers to take off "anger, rage, malice, slander" and to put on "compassion, kindness, humility" (Col. 3:8, 12; see vv. 5–24 NIV). Meditation involves engaging with Scripture on the one hand and prayerfully learning to turn away from meditations of the flesh on the other.

## You're Already Meditating. Why Not Do It Better?

Jesus loved his friends, and it says much about how close he was with one family that he chose their home as his base during the last week before his death. You've heard of this family; there was a brother named Lazarus, raised from the dead by Jesus, and two sisters, Mary and Martha. On one of his visits, we're told that Mary "sat before the Master, hanging on every word he said" (Luke 10:38–40 MSG). Jesus spoke appreciatively of her active listening; her attitude has become a picture of meditation for Christians. Christian meditation involves listening with a heart aware of the presence of Jesus and ready to obey.

It is crucial to make it clear that we already meditate. We think about and obsess over things

Let us mourn before the Lord that we have misplaced our meditation; for the heart of man is restless, it is like the weight of a clock, that will never leave going down as long as it is wound up; the heart of man will always be meditating of something or other; like millstones, if they once grind, they will grind one another; the heart of man will always be grinding, always musing, always meditating on something or other: Now mourn before God heartily, and go into your closets and bemoan it...you have been meditating all your lives long upon vain things, and have not meditated upon the things of eternity, those things that do most concern you; you have been meditating upon trifles, upon things that will not profit at the hour of death, and forgot to meditate of those things that are of eternal [importance].

Edmund Calamy

we care about. At one level, we need to learn how to meditate on helpful subjects rather than simply learn to meditate. Adults know how to talk but often need to learn to communicate in healthy and constructive ways. Likewise, we may need to learn how to use the human tendency to brood, obsess, worry, and daydream as a way to engage with Scripture in a life-giving way. Years ago, I stumbled on this sage advice: "Pray as you can, and do not try to pray as you can't." I invite you to take seriously our Lord's desire for you to meditate on the Bible, his creation, and his acts of redeeming love and grace. That is God's desire for you. He desires that you meditate and dwell on these good things. But do not try to be a spiritual hero: meditate as you can, not as you can't. Join the great adventure of learning to abide in his Word with him.

In the Bible, meditation is seen as a universal human trait of mulling over, thinking about, obsessing, or daydreaming about things that matter to us. The broad category of meditation includes mental activities like worry, focusing on a disliked political figure, savoring the pleasures of life, and displays of character, strength, and virtue. In this book, we look at a subcategory of meditation: intentional meditation on the Bible. Biblical meditation is an open-hearted and relaxed engagement of Scripture in the presence of Christ to enable us to grow in grace and to be more inclined to glorify God and love others.

# –4–

# Meditation and Jesus' Spiritual Formation

> When we meditate on a saying or scene of the Gospel, we do not meditate on a text but on him of whom the text treats and to whom it points: the person of Jesus Christ.
>
> Hans Urs von Balthasar

In an inauspicious house in Caesarea, the church underwent a dramatic change. Cornelius, a Roman soldier, and his household were converted, becoming the first Gentiles in the church. Their conversion was not a quiet affair but dramatic—the Spirit came upon them, and they spoke in tongues just as the apostles had done on Pentecost. Peter explained to those gathered that, "God plays no favorites" (Acts 10:34 MSG). This means that no ethnic, cultural, or geographic barriers stand in the way of anyone receiving forgiveness and new life in Christ. After Peter announced the expansiveness of the Gospel, he gave a concise summary of Jesus' life and ministry.

## He Went Around Doing Good

"You know what has happened throughout the province of Judea, beginning in Galilee after the baptism that John preached—how God anointed Jesus

Meditation is the intensification...
of the Word. It is like bringing the
diffused rays of the sun to a focal
point with a convex lens so that the
heat can be felt in all its intensity.

Simon Chan

of Nazareth with the Holy Spirit and power, and how he went around doing good and healing all who were under the power of the devil, because God was with him" (Acts 10:37–38 NIV).

In his summary, Peter gave a thumbnail sketch of Jesus' life and ministry. He tied Jesus to the ministry of John the Baptist, suggesting they were both part of a single effort by God to reach his people. Then he told how God anointed Jesus of Nazareth for his work as the Messiah, not with oil like the kings of Israel and Judah (think of Samuel anointing David) but with the Holy Spirit and power.

Thus anointed, Jesus went around doing good and healing many who were tyrannized by the devil. Peter summarized Jesus' death and resurrection by saying, "They killed him, hung him from a cross. But in three days God had him up, alive, and out where he could be seen" (Acts 10:39–43 MSG).

Jesus grew into the kind of person whose life could be captured by saying he went about just naturally doing good. Jesus was the Son of God, and as the Nicene Creed says, he was "very God of very God" and "of one substance with the Father." He possessed the divine nature fully and lived a sinless life. It is natural, then, to wonder in what sense Jesus "developed" in his spiritual life. Luke tells us that "Jesus grew in wisdom and in stature and in favor with God and all the people" (Luke 2:52 NLT). Through Jesus' constant prayer, patient suffering, meditation, and obedience to Scripture, God gave him a growing spiritual life, so that the New Testament says of him that he "learned obedience from what he suffered" (Heb. 5:8 NIV). His perfect obedience and wise living did not eliminate growth, but it seemingly accelerated it.

Simply meditate, as far as you are able, on the life and mysteries of Jesus Christ.

Jean-Pierre de Caussade

# Jesus' Spiritual Formation

In thinking about Jesus' spiritual formation, we need to begin with the family in which God, in his providence, placed him. The Gospels portray Mary and Joseph as faithful and pious Jews. When Gabriel visits Mary to announce that she will be the mother of the Messiah, he tells her that she is highly favored and that the Lord is with her. He also tells her not to be afraid because "you have found favor with God" (Luke 1:30 NIV).

After Gabriel told Mary that she was going to bear the Messiah, she traveled to spend time with her relative Elizabeth, who was pregnant with John the Baptist. Elizabeth praised Mary for her faith, and Mary responded with what is now known as the Magnificat, "My soul doth magnify the Lord" (Luke 1:46 KJV). A table in the appendix (page 136) shows clear relationships between Mary's Song of praise (Luke 1:46-55) and the Old Testament, especially the Psalms. There are a couple dozen clear connections between her song and the Old Testament. In her song, Mary revealed herself to be a woman soaked in Scripture, and presumably she had meditated on the passages she alluded to. It is also noteworthy that Mary knew the Psalms deeply. It was the Old Testament book Jesus quoted most often and the book he prayed when he was on the cross. As Peter Williams observed, Mary was a woman of the Book. "The mother that God chose for Jesus was immersed in the Scriptures."

Matthew describes Joseph as a "righteous man" (Matt. 1:19 NRSV). Jesus was born into a poor, pious

In his Gospel, Luke portrays Mary, the mother of Jesus, as a person who practiced the art of meditation. The Holy Spirit made her pregnant with Jesus when the angel spoke the Word of God to her. When she heard the Word of God, it did not go in one ear and out of the other. Instead, she truly heard it and kept it in her heart (Luke 2:19; cf. 11:28)...When the angel announced the conception of Jesus to Mary, she accepted the Word of God, even though she did not understand it. She trusted the will of God...This picture of Mary as a model of meditation is sketched out more fully in two other places. In 2:19 Luke tells us that Mary "treasured up" the words of Christ's birth, "pondering them in her heart." She realized that there was much more to the birth of her son than met her naked eye. She therefore kept puzzling over what had happened to her in the light of the shepherds' report about the message from the angels. She tried to make sense of it for herself by mulling over it and reviewing the whole story in her mind. The same thing happened after Jesus had been left behind at the temple. Luke tells us that Joseph and Mary did not "understand" what Jesus had said about Himself then (2:50). Yet Mary sensed that it was a matter of great importance to her personally. So she "treasured up" these words "in her heart" (2:51). She kept recalling them and paid careful attention to them over a long period of time so as to clarify her relationship with this strange son of hers.

John Kleinig

family of royal lineage who brought him up "in the discipline and instruction of the Lord" (Eph. 6:4 NRSV). Spiritual formation begins in the home before children walk and talk. Jesus was raised in a godly home and was brought up in the synagogue, where he learned the Scriptures. His formation began in a faithful family and community where he learned the Scriptures and the path of righteousness.

The piety of Jesus' parents expressed itself in action. To underscore the type of home in which Jesus was nurtured, Luke tells us that they participated in three Jewish ceremonies when Jesus was born. The first was Jesus' circumcision on the eighth day (Luke 2:21). At his circumcision, he was given the name Jesus. The second was Mary's purification, thirty-three days after his circumcision. The third ceremony was Jesus' presentation in the temple. As Luke says, "Joseph and Mary took him to Jerusalem to present him to the Lord" (Luke 2:22 NIV). Mary also seems to have made a special offering of her child to God for his service, as Hannah had given Samuel to God at the tabernacle. It is during this visit that the two aged righteous ones, Simeon and Anna, blessed Jesus and prophesied concerning his mission and ministry.

Jesus was providentially placed in a home that took his spiritual growth seriously and used the ordinary means of grace (parental love, spiritual faithfulness, participation in the worshiping community) to foster his spiritual development. He learned the Scriptures and learned, as we will see, to meditate on them.

Through Scripture reading, we expose ourselves to the text. Through Scripture meditation, we allow the text to soak into us; we permit the influence or power of Scripture to act within. Isaiah proclaimed God's message: "My word...shall not return empty" (Is 55:10-11). Jeremiah pictured God's word as a "fire" (Jer 5:14; 20:9) and a "hammer that breaks a rock in pieces" (Jer 23:29). The psalmist speaks of it as warning a person (Ps 19:11). "The word of the Lord came to..." is a common biblical phrase that denotes that the word has become a powerful guiding reality in someone. Scripture meditation, then, is a way to cultivate an openness to the word so that "the word of the Lord comes" to you. This is perhaps akin to what the Virgin Mary did as she "pondered" in her heart the implications of Christ's incarnation (Luke 1:26-38).

James C. Wilhoit and Evan B. Howard

## Evidence of His Formation

Another glimpse of Jesus' pious family came when he was twelve. Luke tells us, "Every year Jesus' parents went to Jerusalem for the Festival of the Passover" (Luke 2:41 NIV). Men were required to attend this festival, though it was a practice that had largely been abandoned in Jesus' day. The journey from Nazareth took four or five days in each direction, traveling in a caravan with family and friends. When the family headed back, Jesus turned up missing, and that resulted in a frantic multi-day search for Jesus.

Mary and Joseph found Jesus in the temple, sitting at the feet of the teachers. He assumed the posture of a student and a listener; he entered into a discussion with the teachers. This is the only place Luke portrays Jesus as receiving instruction from Jewish teachers. Luke tells us, "Everyone who heard him was amazed at his understanding and his answers" (Luke 2:47 NIV). He sat with the intelligentsia of his day, Jerusalem's PhDs, for three days, and they were impressed. What were they impressed with? They marveled at "his understanding and his answers," which hints at his practice of meditation. He knew Scripture well and had a profound grasp of its message. The teachers were amazed; they did not dismiss his handling of Scripture. "Their amazement must relate to his deducing things from scripture which they had never found before."

## Jesus' Practice of Meditation

We can infer that the adolescent Jesus was already practicing meditation, which gave him a remarkable functional grasp of Scripture and predisposed him

According to Psalm 1, meditation promises at least three things. The first is stability. The person experienced in meditation is like a tree rooted so that wind cannot blow it away. Notice that this tree is planted by streams of water. Trees by streams do well even if there is little rain. This is an image of someone who can keep going in hard, dry times. We need to have the roots of our heart and soul in God at such times, and meditation is the way to do that. The streams of water represent the "law of the Lord," the Word of God, and to put roots into the water is a metaphor for meditation. Meditation, then, is what gives you stability, peace, and courage in times of great difficulty, adversity, and upheaval. It helps you stay rooted in divine "water" when all other sources of moisture—of joy, hope, and strength—dry up.

Tim Keller

to obey Scripture. One commentator writing on this visit to the temple suggested what Jesus' mastery of Scripture shows us.

> ...The understanding with which his mind grasped and combined thoughts and thus his "answers" with which he replied to the questions addressed to him, which revealed this inner grasp of the truth. These rabbis had never met such a boy. This was...a mind that was filled with the heavenly wisdom of God's Word and truth beyond that of these learned rabbis, yet all unassuming and only eager to learn.

Jesus and his family showed a pattern of obedience to the Law. In the Sermon on the Mount, Jesus said that his mission was not to set aside the Law; rather, "Do not think that I have come to abolish the Law or the Prophets; I have not come to abolish them but to fulfill them" (Matt. 5:17 NIV). Since the Law contains a command to meditate on the Law itself (Josh. 1:8; Deut. 6:5–9), we can assume meditation was something Jesus practiced and was part of his home life. We know of his mother's meditation on the events of his life: "And his mother stored all these things in her heart" (Luke 2:51 NLT). As noted earlier, Mary also appears to have had a deep understanding of the Bible, especially the Psalms.

The four Gospel accounts do not record other events of Jesus' adolescence and young adulthood, so we do not know the specifics of Jesus' life during these years. We can infer that the skills, spiritual practices, and character traits he brought into his ministry were developed during this time. When he entered his public ministry, he had a remarkable command of Scripture.

...in informational reading we seek to grasp the control, to master the text... formational reading: it is to allow the text to master you. In reading the Bible, this means we come to the text with an openness to hear, to receive, to respond, to be a servant of the Word rather than a master of the text...Formational reading, however, requires time to "center down," to use the old Quaker phrase, to become still, to relinquish, to let go of your life in the presence of God.

Robert Mulholland

The Old Testament was seemingly at his fingertips, ready for use. He used seventeen Old Testament stories to illustrate his teaching and to bolster his arguments. His teaching is filled with allusions to the Scriptures; he quotes from memory eighteen different Old Testament passages from fourteen different books; 10 percent of his recorded teachings are either Old Testament quotations or allusions. Kimball notes how his vast grasp of the Hebrew Bible enriched his teaching:

> "Yet he frequently offered interpretations of Scripture that were radically different from the other teachers of his day because of his superior understanding of Scripture...he expounded the OT with an authority that impressed even his religious opponents, the trained Bible teachers of his day."

Joachim Jeremias, in his comprehensive portrayal of Jesus in his *New Testament Theology*, wrote about the role of the Old Testament in Jesus' discipleship: "Jesus lived in the Old Testament. His sayings are incomprehensible unless we recognize this. His last word, according to Mark, was the beginning of Psalm 22, prayed in his Aramaic mother tongue... Numerically, literal and free quotations from the Psalter predominate on the lips of Jesus, and this was evidently his prayer book." The fact that he "lived in the Old Testament," and that the Psalter "was evidently his prayer book" points to the meditation-based spiritual formation he underwent.

On five occasions in the Gospel of Matthew, Jesus challenged his detractors with the question, "Haven't you read?" (see Matt. 12:3, 5; 19:4; 21:16,

Our anxieties and injuries, our aversions and haunting phobias occupy us and demand our attention. But, most of all, we are occupied with the things that we want for ourselves. And we dwell on them day and night. In his commentary on Psalm 1, Luther reflects that those who do not love God or desire His Word do not meditate on it. Instead, "they meditate on other things, namely, on things in which their delight is rooted, things they themselves desire and love, such as gold [money], honor, and flesh [sex]."

John Kleinig

42; 22:31 NIV). He followed this question by relating an Old Testament story or quotation relevant to the situation. When the Pharisees complained that his disciples were plucking grain on the Sabbath (Matt. 12:1–2), Jesus gave a twofold reply, first by asking, "Haven't you read what David did when he and his companions were hungry?" (Matt. 12:3 NIV, referring to 1 Sam. 21:6), and then, "Or haven't you read in the Law that the priests on Sabbath duty in the temple desecrate the Sabbath and yet are innocent?" (Matt. 12:5 NIV, referring to Num. 28:8, 10). Notice what Jesus was doing as he applied these Scriptures to the controversy at hand. He used an understanding of the passage that had come by careful thought about its context and meaning. He called his opponents to read and understand the Scriptures more fully. He demonstrated how the insight from meditating on, studying, contemplating, and pondering the Scriptures enables one to see its rich and life-giving message.

This grasp of Scripture came through his program of study and meditation on the Scriptures. John quoted Jesus' opponents with apparent approval: "How does he know so much without being schooled?" (John 7:15 MSG). He engaged in debates with the intellectual leaders and had a deep knowledge of the Scriptures, which he could effortlessly access. Jesus could read Hebrew (Luke 4:17–20) and would have had access to the Scriptures in synagogues, but presumably he did not have his own copy. His quotations from Scripture were from memory and showed a depth of personalized understanding that is the unmistakable fruit of meditation.

... humbly accept the word God has planted in your hearts, for it has the power to save your souls.

James 1:21 NLT

Jesus overcame the devil through his skillful use of Scripture. Luke tells us that Jesus, "full of the Holy Spirit" (Luke 4:1 NIV), was led by the Spirit into the wilderness, where the devil tempted him. For forty days, there was a spiritual battle, and it seems to have reached its climax in the three temptations: make bread out of stones; spectacularly jump from a pinnacle and rely on angels to break the fall; worship Satan in return for all the kingdoms of the world. Jesus answered these temptations with the bold use of Scripture.

One of the first things to note about Jesus is that he loved to minister to people, but he was distrustful of the praise of the crowds. He was constantly slipping away for prayer and solitude, not to check his phone or just chill. Luke sums up this tendency by telling us that the crowds were swarming, "But Jesus often withdrew to lonely places and prayed" (Luke 5:16 NIV). And when the Pharisees were furious with him, Luke says that Jesus' response was to go out alone to the mountain to pray through the night (Luke 6:12).

It was his regular practice to attend the synagogue on the Sabbath (Luke 4:16), where he would no doubt join with the rest in the prayers and worship and hear the Scriptures read. He realized that his mission was given by the Father and was not to be found by listening to the crowds, so he was up early praying and meditating and constantly abiding with the Father.

### Meditation Enabled Jesus Not to Waste His Trials

The author of Hebrews emphasizes Jesus' formation through his suffering, which brought about his maturation. "Son though he was, he learned

There are not many rules, but one everlasting and unchangeable rule to live by. For this reason...David's statement that the life of a righteous man is a continual meditation upon the law [Ps. 1:2]...is just as applicable to every age, even to the end of the world.

John Calvin

obedience from what he suffered and, once made perfect, he became the source of eternal salvation for all who obey him" (Heb. 5:8–9 NIV).

Listen to how the Messiah is described in Isaiah 53: "He was despised and rejected by men, a man of sorrows and acquainted with grief...he was despised, and we esteemed him not....Stricken, smitten by God, and afflicted....He was crushed for our iniquities.... He was oppressed, and he was afflicted" (Isa. 53:3–5, 7 ESV). Without bitterness or complaining, Jesus used his suffering for his maturation.

We know about Jesus' practice of voluntary spiritual disciplines (meaning disciplines he chose to do), like prayer, fasting, meditation, and worship. Perhaps as significant for Jesus' spiritual formation was his participation in what we might call involuntary disciplines (his wise response to trials). These would include responding wisely to criticism, opposition, betrayals, grumbling and plotting directed at him. Jesus did not waste his trials. Again, notice how the writer to Hebrews captures this: "During the days of Jesus' life on earth, he offered up prayers and petitions with fervent cries and tears..., and he was heard because of his reverent submission" (Heb 5:7 NIV). Note the reality of the pain and suffering Jesus faced, shown in "fervent cries and tears," and observe the evidence of his spiritual formation: "he was heard because of his reverent submission." He was heard, but not simply because he was the Son of God and the Father had no choice but to listen to him. No, he had grown to the point that his approach to God could be called "reverent submission."

As you move from reading to meditation, you are seeking to saturate and immerse yourself in the Word, to luxuriate in its living waters, and to receive the words as an intimate and personal message from God. The purpose of meditation is to penetrate the Scriptures and to let them penetrate us through the loving gaze of the heart.

Kenneth Boa

Why does this matter? The writer to Hebrews thought it was important for us to realize that Jesus faced struggles and temptations as we do. We all know the power of discovering that someone understands what we are going through, that someone knows the pain we are experiencing: facing the struggles of loving a mentally ill sibling, a betrayal by a close friend, the loss of a dream.

Jesus is not a porcelain figure with a painted-on perpetual smile. Here are a few of the things Jesus experienced: he was homeless; he experienced a sympathetic crowd turning on him and trying to kill him; his family said, "He is out of his mind" (Mark 3:21 NIV); he dealt with the death of close friends; he endured gossip and slander; his close followers didn't understand his message; he endured separation from God. In whatever hard situation you find yourself— opposition, mental distress, interpersonal strife, or physical suffering—Jesus experienced these too, and he models how they can be used for our spiritual growth. So don't waste your trials—your financial pressure, family pain, relational tension, or health challenge. Instead, learn from Jesus the power of involuntary disciplines. We have seen that Jesus used Scripture in his trials (such as his temptation and his crucifixion), and I believe his ability to use Scripture is the result of his meditation practice.

Psalm 119 focuses on the Word of God and clarifies that there is a deep connection between meditation and suffering, especially in the pain of interpersonal conflict. "May the arrogant be put to shame for wronging me without cause; but I will meditate on your precepts" (Ps. 119:78 NIV). "It was good for me to be afflicted so that I might learn your decrees"

In the timeless story of Mary and Martha, these sisters offer a poignant example of two styles of thinking: distraction versus attentive awareness. Martha, while preparing a meal for Jesus and his disciples, was "distracted by her many tasks," while Mary "sat at the Lord's feet." Martha subsequently complained to Jesus: "Lord, do you not care that my sister has left me to do all the work by myself?" Her complaint seems fair, but Jesus surprisingly defended Mary: "Martha, Martha, you are worried and distracted by many things; there is need of only one thing. Mary has chosen the better part, which will not be taken away from her" (Luke 10:38–42). But here we see Jesus call us to also carve out time to sit quietly and listen, even when it seems there is no time for it. So often, our being, even more than our doing, is what connects us to the heart of God.

Irene Kraegel

(Ps. 119:71 NIV). Jesus showed a pattern of dwelling on God's Word in the face of opposition and that contributed to his "reverent submission" to God.

## Jesus' Deep Working Knowledge of Scripture

After Jesus' resurrection, he met two followers on the road to Emmaus. They were downcast because of Jesus' crucifixion. Without revealing his identity to them, "Jesus took them through the writings of Moses and all the prophets, explaining from all the Scriptures the things concerning himself" (Luke 24:27 NLT). When Luke says that Jesus explained to them all the things about himself throughout the Bible, he means that Jesus gave them the through line, the whole story of redemption. "Then he started at the beginning, with the Books of Moses, and went on through all the Prophets, pointing out everything in the Scriptures that referred to him" (Luke 24:25–27 MSG). Jesus told the story of redemption in a way that captivated them. Afterward, they said to each other, "Were not our hearts burning within us while he talked with us on the road and opened the Scriptures to us?" (Luke 24:32 NIV). He found learners eager to understand the events that had turned their world upside down. He did this from memory, without notes or a Bible, because he had meditated and memorized these portions of Scripture and knew them like the back of his hand, for they were deep in his heart. He pondered the Scripture that was read in public worship and that he read on his own, and he used it in his ongoing conversation with his Father. We can slip away to a quiet spot to pray and meditate and, in this way, imitate Jesus' pattern.

# – 5 –

# Meditating on Scripture

Study this Book of Instruction continually.
Meditate on it day and night so you will
be sure to obey everything written in it.
Only then will you prosper and succeed
in all you do.

Joshua 1:8 NLT

I have come to enjoy baking four-ingredient artisan bread that uses water, flour, yeast, and salt. The recipe I use is simple, and I have come to savor the results—a wonderful aroma, an attractive crusty appearance, and an inviting chewy texture. My mother was a bread baker, and the appeal of the smell and texture of freshly baked bread was seemingly imprinted on me early on. In the New York Times, I read how easily one could bake bread with just four ingredients and without kneading. I wanted to try it, and now I am hooked. I hope this explanation of meditation gives you a sense that meditation is simple, like baking simple bread. It is not some complex gourmet spiritual practice for elites.

The word is very near you...

Deut. 30:14 NIV


The word is near you...

Rom. 10:8 NIV

## The Biblical Command to Meditate

Set forth in the law of Israel was an expectation that Israelites would meditate on God's Word. "Hear, O Israel: The Lord our God, the Lord is one" (Deut. 6:4 NIV) is known as the Shema, the central theological passage in the Old Testament. Immediately after this statement the Israelites were told, "And you must commit yourselves wholeheartedly to these commands that I am giving you today. Repeat them again and again to your children. Talk about them when you are at home and when you are on the road, when you are going to bed and when you are getting up" (Deut. 6:6–7 NLT). This passage is a picture of Bible engagement, talking about and repeating the Law; this was an expectation Moses gave to all Israel. In Joshua 1:8 and Psalm 1:2, we find the call to meditate on God's Law given to those who want to flourish. The command to meditate is given without exceptions. It is not for just men, or priests, or kings, or parents. It is the pathway of blessing for all. God in his grace commands what is within our reach with his help.

Meditation is a life-giving way of relating to God through Scripture that can be done anywhere by anyone. In our culture, meditation is portrayed as an elite activity requiring training or done in special centers for those with time to spare. In the Bible, meditation could be done in a field (Gen. 24:63), wherever one went (Josh. 1:7–8), in the temple (Ps. 48:9), day and night (Ps. 1:2), in times of conflict (Ps. 119:23), at night (Ps. 77:6), and in bed (Ps. 63:6). A friend, as he was recovering from a heart transplant, described with deep appreciation how he was taught to meditate on spiritual truths by a hospital chaplain.

From a commentary on Philippians 4:8

Finally, brothers and sisters, whatever is true, whatever is noble, whatever is right, whatever is pure, whatever is lovely, whatever is admirable—if anything is excellent or praiseworthy—think about such things. (Phil. 4:8, NIV)

"Consider" or "think on" (logizesthe) means "meditate on" or "mull over"...The invitation/command is literally to fill the mind with these virtues. Paul is an astute psychologist and knows that the greatest area of sin is that of thought, and so he gives "alternatives" to sinful or even useless or trivial or petty thoughts.

Bonnie Thurston and Judith Ryan

Several young parents have mentioned learning to meditate as they sat up late with a fussy infant. One friend described how his jail cell became his monastery as he learned to meditate on the Bible. Meditation is simple—not simplistic or easy, but available to all who seek to meet God in this way. One image of meditation in the New Testament is that of a nursing newborn baby: "Like newborn babies, you must crave pure spiritual milk so that you will grow" (1 Pet. 2:2 NLT). As soon as we are born again in Christ, we have the equipment to meditate and take in the life-giving Word of God.

I mentioned my four-ingredient bread. I suggest that biblical meditation has four elements (easily remembered using the acronym PROD). These are not steps but ingredients (like flour and water in bread) that you should use in your meditation recipe.

*Present:* We meditate in the presence of God. Our risen Lord promised always to be present with his disciples: "And be sure of this: I am with you always, even to the end of the age" (Matt. 28:20 NLT). Paul tells us we are spiritually united with Jesus: Christ is in us (2 Cor. 13:5), and we are in him (1 Cor. 1:30). In meditating, we interact with our risen Lord Jesus and are strengthened, challenged, comforted, and guided by him. The fact that we are fellowshipping with Christ is a distinctive aspect of biblical meditation.

*Read:* We engage in a slow, repetitive oral reading of Scripture. The Hebrew words translated as "meditate" in the Bible have root meanings of "sing, coo, growl, mutter, or hum." Make it physical: read aloud, mutter, make up a song or write the passage down, engage your body in the reading process, and read very slowly.

Read the text, re-read it, re-read it and read it again. Turn it over and over in your mind, like Mary the mother of Jesus who wondered at all the things the shepherds had told her, pondering them in her heart. Probe your text, like a bee with a spring blossom, or like a hummingbird probing a hibiscus flower for its nectar. Worry at it like a dog with a bone. Suck it as a child sucks an orange. Chew it as a cow chews the cud.

John Stott

*Open-hearted:* There are great promises made to those who meditate: "You [will] prosper and succeed in all you do" (Josh. 1:8 NLT; see also Ps. 1:3). The positive change that flows from meditation comes from God working in and with us. Meditation is always a cooperative venture. We are in a listening partnership with God as we sit with his Word. This is not an activity you will master by sheer willpower and perseverance; it is a way of opening yourself to Christ through his Word and truth. Enter into meditation with the attentive posture that you'd bring to any important conversation.

*Delight:* Meditation grows out of an attraction to and respect for the Word of God. We meditate on what we care about. A delight in the Bible is something that comes as a gift from God that we should seek in prayer. Delight also develops as we read with a sense of marvel and attentiveness to the literary beauty of the Bible. Since meditation is delight-driven pondering, we should start meditating on the Scriptures we already find attractive. The Shepherd Psalm (Ps. 23), the Lord's Prayer (Matt. 6:9–13), or God's declaration of love (John 3:16) are favorites of many. It's best to start off with what we delight in already.

## What Does Meditation Look Like?

Meditation is as simple as saying a verse of Scripture back to God in a low voice. That is the essential move in biblical meditation. Remember, there are two sides to meditation. One is engaging with the Word of God; the other is not getting wrapped up in worries, obsessions, political rumination, self-attacking thoughts, and social comparison. A time-

Meditation may be thus described: it is a holy exercise of the mind; whereby we bring the truths of God to remembrance, and do seriously ponder upon them and apply them to ourselves.

Thomas Watson

tested strategy to walk away from negative thinking is to have a word of Scripture, a mental picture of beauty, or a deep truth ready at hand. If you are distracted, switch your attention, and meditate on your prepared word, picture, or truth. Do not try to suppress negative thoughts; turn from them to the "true, noble, right, pure, lovely, admirable, excellent, or praiseworthy" (see Phil. 4:8 NIV).

I was in a crowded arena fifty years ago when I was first introduced to meditating on Scripture. I took the call given by the speaker to meditate quite seriously, and after the seminar, I immediately worked on memorizing Psalm 1. I was told that was the passage that explained the process of meditation. I thought at the time that I made a valiant effort to meditate, but it would be decades before biblical meditation became a life-giving habit.

As I reflect on that first experiment with meditation, I am now struck how I took it on as a project, like so many projects done in my own power. I do not think I ever prayed for guidance on how to meditate, and I know I had no sense that Jesus, the Master Meditator, could teach me so much. One of my friends and co-learners dubbed meditation "biblical self-talk," and we liked that moniker. We had a good deal of pride and an almost magical view of how God uses the Bible to sanctify his people. We were practicing a homespun form of cognitive self-therapy. We figured that meditation largely consisted in saying words of truth to yourself, and that you would change with a large enough dose. We meditated on a Bible that we viewed as a collection of facts that were essential to get inside our brains. In those days, I was partial to meditating on Paul's epistles, saying

May these words of my mouth and this
meditation of my heart
be pleasing in your sight,
LORD, my Rock and my Redeemer.

Ps. 19:14 NIV

verses repeatedly with no recognition that I was doing this in God's presence or that my heart and affections might be involved in this process.

I now see meditation as analogous to a four-strand rope made up of the four elements of PROD. In my early days of meditation, my practice was but a single thin thread. I had a simple, heady way of repeating Scripture and, quite frankly, I think I was hoping for a magical result. One of my friends in this era joked, "A verse a day keeps the devil away." We did not really believe that slogan, but my meditation was closer to being a charm or a talisman than I realized.

What has been my path to a more fulsome way of meditating? It certainly was not a linear and predictable one. Perhaps, first, there was the gracious call of God; I can identify the intersection in Evanston, Illinois, where it happened. I was given the desire to read Scripture for spiritual refreshment, not to read out of duty or to be informed, but to be refreshed by God. Then, there was a season of profound brokenness where I saw the depth of my anger and my inability to remove it. In my neediness, I sensed the reality of my hunger for God. I learned deeply, what Dallas Willard so often quipped, "God's address is at-the-end-your-rope.com." I began to read Scripture with a renewed sense that I needed the guidance it alone could provide. My theological training gave me a deep intellectual certainty about my union with Christ. Through contemplative prayer, I began to experience the reality of a verse I had memorized years before. "I have been crucified with Christ and I no longer live, but Christ lives in me. The life I now live in the body, I live by faith in the Son of God, who loved me and gave himself for me" (Gal. 2:20 NIV). I am actually united

Our "being still" as Christians is almost the opposite of the Eastern forms of meditation. Its purpose is not to reach a certain emotional state, but rather to enjoy an intimate relationship with Jesus Christ in order to become more and more like him (Romans 8:29). We do not want to meet with ourselves, we want to meet with God. Being still before God is not looking inward, introspection, but looking upward, inspiration.

Pablo Martinez

to Christ, and I can turn to him throughout the day. One result of this growing realization is that I found myself touching my heart throughout the day as a reminder that Christ dwells in me (Col. 1:27). Many factors led to my practice of meditation deepening. My study of meditation in the Bible showed it to be an embodied activity that involves the whole person. I also learned patterns of present moment awareness and greater focus through mindfulness meditation, which have helped me be more present with the text and God in my meditation.

I am fully convinced that God has called us to meditate on his Word, and this pursuit is part of the Christian's vocation, chewing on the Word and thereby taking it to heart. In the psalms, to know a person meditates is to see that they are a righteous person: someone who honors God, keeps commitments, respects the vulnerable, and cherishes this very moment as a gift. As you seek to grow in your meditation practice, remember, "Always we begin again." In prayer, we ask Jesus to teach us and guide us in our meditation, and we look for those who can teach us to meditate. These are Christ-followers, who keep commitments, are grateful, respect the vulnerable, and cherish this present moment as a gift.

# – 6 –

# Meditation:
# The Pathway of Life

Have you not realized that most of your
unhappiness in life is due to the fact that
you are listening to yourself instead of
talking to yourself?

Martyn Lloyd Jones

Listening to yourself and talking to yourself
are so very different. One is more like overhearing
gossip, and the other is like speaking a true word of
affirmation. One leaves a dirty residue on you, while
the other builds you up. Consider those negative self-
critical thoughts that greet you when you wake up.
Where did they come from? The trials of yesterday,
sins once confessed but now assailing you, self-
doubts; you are not the conscious author of them.
They just arise as the self talks to the self. I spoke with
a young woman about the effects her self-criticism
had on her, and she said, "I read that these are called
automatic negative thoughts, and I can't do anything
about them." I disagree. I think you can do something
about these negative thoughts. At a minimum you can
form a different relationship with them.

The difference between talking to yourself and
listening to yourself is the issue of intentionality.
Negative and self-critical thoughts flood our minds.

77

Another common form of spontaneous meditation is worrying. No one that I know decides to worry. Like daydreaming, worrying is something that happens to us. When we worry, we imagine the worst things that could happen to us and to those whom we love. Scenarios of trouble and disaster run through our minds repeatedly and obsessively, like a video loop...We also meditate spontaneously when a piece of music or the verse of a song hooks into our minds and replays itself there repeatedly, whether we enjoy it or not.

John Kleinig

They are unbidden and seem to be automatic. You need to pause and recognize that not every thought is true or worth entertaining. So, you, in essence, say, "Self, listen up for a moment; I have something to say to you." And then speak a good and true word to yourself: "I am a child of God," "I am blessed," "I am fearfully and wonderfully made," or "I am chosen and loved." Speak true and affirming words to challenge the negative thoughts.

## Meditation Involves Showing Hospitality to the Word

I grew up in a family where showing hospitality and welcoming those on the margin was a way of life. While I was at home, this often involved inviting people for a meal. Later in life, my mother's hospitality centered on her sewing machine as she invited people over for her to help with their sewing projects or clothing repairs. She always gave attention to making her home a welcoming place—a place of warm hospitality.

We are to show hospitality to God's Word and welcome it into our lives. In the Book of James, we are told, "So get rid of all the filth and evil in your lives, and humbly accept the word God has planted in your hearts, for it has the power to save your souls" (James 1:21 NLT). James calls us to follow the tried-and-true New Testament pattern of taking off and putting on. In Paul's language, this means "putting on the Lord Jesus Christ, and not organizing our lives around the satisfaction of our natural desires" (Rom. 13:14 author's translation). We lay aside our old self and "put on the new self, created to be like God in

When your words came, I
ate them; they were my joy
and my heart's delight, for I
bear your name, LORD God
Almighty.

Jer. 15:16 NIV

true righteousness and holiness" (Eph. 4:24 NIV). We are to accept with a teachable spirit the word of truth that God has planted in us through the new birth. We are to prepare our hearts to be supple and open to the Word God has planted in his grace. It is the "saving word." Since James is writing to Christians when he speaks of the Word saving them, he is not talking about their conversion but speaking of the Word's power to heal and restore.

Showing hospitality to the Word also means we appreciate its authority, beauty, and value as a guide. The world is hostile to the Bible, and our culture's skepticism and intellectual doubts can easily rub off on us. For the Bible to become a place where we meet God, we need to set aside our guardedness toward it and receive it warmly.

## Meditation Involves Calming and Quieting Our Souls

One of the great joys of parenting small children is the pleasure of them snuggling in one's lap just to be close. David paints a word picture of his relationship with God by comparing himself to a child who wants to snuggle close. The psalm opens with David reminding himself that he has set aside lofty thoughts and plans; "Instead, I have calmed and quieted myself, like a weaned child who no longer cries for its mother's milk" (Ps. 131:2 NLT). He is like a well-fed child resting peacefully in his mother's embrace. To come to this place, he has humbled himself and quieted himself.

As I talk with people about barriers to meditation, one of the first things people mention is their noisy

Some people like to read so many chapters every day. I would not dissuade them from the practice, but I would rather lay my soul soaking in half a dozen verses all day than I would, as it were, rinse my hands in several chapters. Oh, to bathe in a text of Scripture and to let it be sucked up into your very soul till it saturates your heart!... Set your heart upon God's Word! It is the only way to know it thoroughly—let your whole nature be plunged into it as cloth into dye.

Charles Spurgeon

mind—the constant ongoing mental conversation. David had learned to calm and quiet himself. We need to slowly train ourselves to shift from the distractions to the quiet presence of God. We do not just try but methodically train, so that "I keep my eyes always on the LORD. With him at my right hand, I will not be shaken" (Ps. 16:8 NIV).

One of the struggles that people notice as they begin to meditate is the presence of distracting or disturbing thoughts. You are not alone in facing this challenge, and Christian writers have given guidance on this topic from the days of the early church to our own. While inattention can be considered a perennial issue, there is growing evidence that our constant use of phones and various digital devices has left us more easily distracted. The broad consensus from Christian spiritual teachers through the centuries is as follows: (1) To set thoughts in order takes long-term training of the mind, not just short-term attempts. (2) To suppress these distracting thoughts or push them down does not work and often makes the problem worse. (3) Finding an anchor, like your breath or a prayer phrase, which you can quickly turn to when you are distracted, can help calm and focus the mind. (4) Learn to turn toward God in humble prayer, asking for the perseverance to cultivate a quiet mind. A nineteenth-century anonymous monk captured this well when writing about becoming free of troubling thoughts when praying: "It is impossible for man to drive out and eradicate the devil's assaults from the heart except by the contrite prayer of the heart."

We all struggle to maintain our focus in meditation. This reality is part of the human condition, but your

For the first period of my Christian life, I thought Christian development was all about thinking harder about things I already knew. It brought some useful results...I read some words of a medieval writer [who]...stressed the importance of meditating on Scripture. Not understanding, but meditating. Here is what he had to say.

> Meditation is the process in which you diligently turn over in your heart whatever you have read or heard, earnestly reflecting upon it and thus enkindling your affections in some particular manner or enlightening your understanding.

These words brought new light and life to my reading of the Bible. I had thought that meditation was some kind of Buddhist practice that was off limits for Christians. Yet I had failed to notice how often Old Testament writers spoke of meditating on God's law. Meditation was about letting the biblical text impact upon me, "enkindling the emotions"—what a wonderful phrase!—and "enlightening the understanding." And my heart, as well as my mind, was to be involved! The worlds of understanding and emotion were brought together, opening the door to a far more authentic and satisfying way of living out the Christian life.

Alister McGrath

particular struggle and your specific thought triggers are unique to you. Our Lord calls us to meditate, so we need to engage in a discipleship program of our minds so that they are calm and quiet enough to engage God's Word. The joy and refreshment of meditation are worth the effort of seeking to be more present-oriented and less buffeted by troubling thoughts. As I look back on my growth in this area, here are a few actions I have found helpful.

Recruit your body. When I first sought to pray for an extended time, I found it impossible. My thoughts wandered like a ball in a pinball machine, and I got sleepy, even after a good night's rest. I hit upon the idea of walking when I prayed, and that helped immensely. The movement and commitment to completing a predetermined route seemed to help me stay focused. When I found my mind wandering, I would take a few seconds to observe my walking and then go back to praying. Later, I made a prayer stool, which I use about a quarter of the time I pray. To use it, I kneel, a posture of reverent submission that helps me realize this time is special. I am used to daydreaming when I sit in a comfortable chair but not when I am on my prayer stool. I write notes during my meditation, I typically light a candle, I begin by drinking a cup of tea, and I always use the same space when at home. Those physical activities help ground me and enhance my concentration.

Bracket the time. You need to set aside your formal meditation time from the rest of your life. I discovered years ago that the best way for me to do this was by setting a timer. When I start the timer, I know I am setting aside this time for special use. Often, I

To this day I suckle at the Lord's Prayer like a child, and as an old man eat and drink from it and never get my fill.

Martin Luther

begin by looking at the chair I will sit in and use the phrase a friend taught me. Speaking on behalf of God, I say, "Jim, I'm glad to see you this morning!" The time is set aside, and I have learned not to entertain inevitable distractions or thoughts. One simple way to bracket your time is to join a meditation group or seek to use your time in the worship service at church for meditation.

Find an anchor for your thoughts. When my mind wanders, I take a moment and just observe my breath. I breathe in through my nose and out through my mouth three or four times, and I pay attention to the physical sensations. When I find myself distracted, I do not beat myself up; I focus on watching my breath, sometimes with a brief prayer of confession. Other times, it is the simple cry of the heart, "Father, I love you," gently repeated several times. Prayerfully seek an anchor for your thoughts to which you can quickly turn.

Be prayerful. God calls us to meditate on his Word, and he is eager to help us grow in this practice. Cry out to God for the strength and insight to clear your mind enough to meditate. We need to train our minds, and God, in his providence, has given us the means to do this through very ordinary means of training. The call to prayer is not a call for us to be passive but a recognition that we cannot master our minds on our own, and Jesus, our ever-present Teacher and Lord, is willing and able to show us what to do.

Finally, in the past fifty years, a great deal has been learned about cognitive processes. You may find

And there is nothing that so much strengthens our faith and trust in God, that so much preserves pureness of the heart and also of outward godly life and conversation, as continual reading and recording of God's word. For that thing which, by continual reading of Holy Scripture, and diligent searching of the same, is deeply printed and graven in the heart, at length turns almost into nature...

Thomas Cranmer

that a counselor or therapist can provide guidance and training to help you become more settled in your thinking and less ruled by troubling thoughts.

# — 7 —

# Meditating in Everyday Life

There is a way of life so hid with Christ in God that in the midst of the day's business one is inwardly lifting brief prayers, short ejaculations of praise, subdued whispers of adoration and of tender love to the Beyond that is within. No one need know about it. I only speak to you because it is a sacred trust, not mine but to be given to others. One can live in a well-nigh continuous state of unworded prayer, directed toward God, directed toward people and enterprises we have on our heart. There is no hurry about it all; it is a life unspeakable and full of glory, an inner world of splendor within which we, unworthy, may live. Some of you know it and live in it; others of you may wistfully long for it; it can be yours.

Thomas Kelly

As you think about developing a meditation practice, keep in mind that you can engage in three types of biblical meditation. These patterns are described in the Bible and have been written about in the literature of Christian spirituality.

But Mary treasured up all these
things and pondered them in her
heart.

Luke 2:19  NIV

## Spontaneous Meditation

The first pattern is spontaneous meditation, and this is something every person does. As I mentioned before, if you find yourself worrying, rehashing an injustice, or caught up in daydreaming about an upcoming event, then you are engaged in spontaneous meditation. The subjects can be positive or negative, so our goal in cultivating spontaneous meditation is to switch our thinking from those things that we are obsessing over to a focus on God's Word and his truth.

Over the centuries, Christians have developed several practices to encourage spontaneous meditation. I encourage you to follow the advice that I gave earlier and meditate as you can, not as you can't. In Psalms 1 and 2, we are shown two types of meditation. One is the spiritually destructive form of worry, lustful and pornographic thoughts, obsessing over past hurts, and planning evil. The second form of meditation focuses on God's truth and his Word. We are all meditators, and we need to wean ourselves from the spiritually unhelpful automatic meditations to a focus on God. Consider Psalm 16, where David writes, "I will praise the Lord, who counsels me; even at night my heart instructs me" (Ps. 16:7 NIV). David has developed a conversational relationship with God. As a result, his heart has been trained so that when he wakes up at night, his thought (that is, his automatic meditations) give him good and life-giving advice.

Since the early church, Christian teachers have encouraged believers to find a prayer that they can have readily at hand so that they are prepared to obey the command to pray constantly. Unceasing prayer is a valuable spiritual practice that we should cultivate.

Finally, brethren, whatever things are true, whatever things are noble, whatever things are just, whatever things are pure, whatever things are lovely, whatever things are of good report, if there is any virtue and if there is anything praiseworthy—meditate on these things.

Phil. 4:8 NKJV

At points, it is indistinguishable from biblical meditation. Continual prayer was so important to Paul that he wrote about it to five communities: the Romans, Ephesians, Philippians, Colossians, and Thessalonians. His letters are filled with an emphasis on his unceasing prayer and in his letters he invited his readers to practice it. He discusses it very matter-of-factly, giving the impression that it is something all Christians can do. Paul tells the Thessalonians to "pray without ceasing" (1 Thess. 5:17 ESV). In his Letter to the Romans, he urges them to "be constant in prayer" (Rom. 12:12 ESV).

The writer to the Hebrews urges his readers to "continually offer to God a sacrifice of praise—the fruit of lips that openly profess his name" (Heb. 13:15 NIV). This imagery reminds us that there was a call for continual prayer in the Old Testament. The psalmist declares, "Seven times a day I praise you for your righteous laws" (Ps. 119:164 NIV), which has long been seen as a call to offer prayer throughout the day. The psalmist calls for continual prayer for the king: "May prayer be made for him continually, and blessings invoked for him all day long" (Ps. 72:15 NRSV). One of the ways to pray constantly is to select a short prayer to pray throughout the day.

John Cassian (c. AD 360–c. 435) was one of the earliest writers who suggested using a prayer phrase. He suggested using Psalm 70:1: "This, then, is the devotional formula proposed to you as absolutely necessary for possessing the perpetual awareness of God: 'O God, come to my assistance; Lord, make haste to help me.' Not without reason has this verse been selected from out of the whole body of scripture. Verse one was a prayer that Christians could have

...a man may take into his understanding and memory more truth in one hour than he is able well to digest in many. A man may eat too much, but he cannot digest too well.

Richard Baxter

readily at hand." Unceasing prayer and meditation go hand in hand, so I encourage you to find a phrase or a short passage of Scripture that you can use to direct your thoughts when there is spare time or when you find yourself tumbling down a rabbit hole of negative thinking.

Choose a prayer word or phrase in prayerful consultation with the Lord, and here be careful and do not fall into prayer phrase envy. A friend or mentor may have a phrase they use, and you may be tempted out of respect for them to adopt it. That might work well for you, or you may find it a bit like David trying to put on Saul's armor. After putting it on, "David tried to walk but he could hardly budge. David told Saul, 'I can't even move with all this stuff on me. I'm not used to this.' And he took it all off" (1 Sam. 17:38–39 MSG). Select a word that the Lord gives you to have readily at hand.

## Prayer Phrases

- But thanks be to God. Rom. 6:17
- Father, glorify your name. John 12:28
- Lord, save me! Matt. 14:30
- What shall I do, Lord? Acts 22:10
- Lord, to whom shall we go? You have the words of eternal life. John 6:68
- Return to me, for I have redeemed you. Isa. 44:22
- I have engraved you on the palms of my hands. Isa. 49:16
- In repentance and rest is your salvation, in

Therefore, holy brothers and sisters, who share in the heavenly calling, fix your thoughts on Jesus, whom we acknowledge as our apostle and high priest.

Heb. 3:1 NIV

quietness and trust is your strength. Isa. 30:15
- He is good; his love endures forever. 2 Chr. 5:13
- Spare your people, LORD. Joel 2:17
- Now strengthen my hands. Neh. 6:9
- LORD, my strength and my fortress. Jer. 16:19
- LORD, the great God. Neh. 8:6
- Hasten, O God, to save me; come quickly, LORD, to help me. Ps. 70:1
- Stop striving. Ps. 46:10
- Your grace is sufficient for me. 2 Cor. 12:9
- Speak, LORD, for Your servant is listening. 1 Sam. 3:9

When selecting a prayer word or phrase, take time to read the phrase in its biblical context so that you understand the full meaning of the passage.

Learn to be comfortable with being bored. The small spaces throughout one's day provide opportunities to turn and ponder the "true, noble, right, pure, lovely, admirable, excellent or praiseworthy" (see Phil. 4:8 NIV). You need to learn to let your mind turn to your passage; if you have trained yourself to pick up your phone, or a book, or begin planning when you have a free moment, you will find it hard to meditate. Let boredom breed meditation.

Another aspect of spontaneous meditation might be called spiritual attentiveness. In the story we know as "Jacob's Ladder," Jacob, in a dream, comes face-to-face with the reality of God. Jacob stops for the night at "a certain place" (Gen. 28:11 NIV), not a

99

When I worked on translating the Book of Proverbs for the New International Version of the Bible, I spent sixty hours a week working to interpret the text in a credible way. But after ten weeks of work, I was farther away from God than when I began, because I forgot to pray that God speak to me.

Bruce Waltke

temple or shrine, but "a good place to set up camp" (Gen. 28:11 NLT), and as he slept, he dreamed of the stairway and heard God's message for him. When he woke up, he said, "Surely the LORD is in this place, and I wasn't even aware of it!" (Gen. 28:17 NLT). "I wasn't aware." A friend of mine who is a therapist mentioned that he spends a great deal of time simply helping people to see what is unfolding in their lives.

The Psalter is divided into several books; the first book (Psalms 1–41) opens with Psalm 1, which describes the happy or blessed person, while the last psalm of this book (Ps. 41) begins with the statement, "Blessed are those" (Ps. 41:1 NIV). Here the blessed person gives thought to those in need. "God's view of good fortune consists of those who take consideration of the helpless." In Psalm 1, the blessed person meditates on the Law, and in Psalm 41, the blessed person uses their renewed mind and soul to consider the helpless. The spontaneous chewing on the Word of God or delighting in God's truth and beauty is intended to take place within a posture of spiritual awareness. In an essay published near the end of his life, C. S. Lewis asks "How, then, it may be asked, can we...avoid Him?...In our own time and place, [avoiding God] is extremely easy. Avoid silence, avoid solitude, avoid any train of thought that leads off the beaten track. Concentrate on money, sex, status, health and (above all) on your own grievances. Keep the radio on. Live in a crowd. Use plenty of sedation."

There have been times when I was in such a stew over an injury by another that I had no headspace left to meditate. Holding grudges, nursing resentments, being fixated on political opponents—these are all forms of meditation. These thought patterns do not

The godly offer good counsel;
    they teach right from wrong.
They have made God's law their own,
    so they will never slip from his path.

Ps. 37:30-31 NLT

produce the fruit of the Spirit in our lives, and they deprive us of the mental space needed to meditate. If a stumbling block to meditation is the mental noise caused by resentment and past wounds, then please do not try harder to clear your mind, but seek out help from a counselor, pastor, or wise friend who can help you deal constructively with your past. We forgive others and seek to reduce resentments so that we can live well and walk in love. Bitterness and its attendant mental clutter make it hard for us to focus on the beautiful and life-giving Word of God. As one person quipped, "Why do you let that obnoxious roommate live rent free in your head?"

## Group and Church Meditation

### Learning to Meditate in Church

Perhaps the single best place to learn Christian meditation is a worship service in church. Groups can also help support your meditation practice, but I have found that church is a great place to learn and practice meditation. "The Divine Service is thus the school for Christian meditation, its proper context. There we receive meditation as a gift. There we learn to meditate for ourselves as the Holy Spirit does His work in us while we listen to God's Word. The beauty of that arrangement is that it requires so little from us in time and effort and ability."

When we are in church, we are already aware that we are in the presence of God. Through worship, our hearts have been opened. We are invited to simply take Scripture that we hear and gently repeat it to ourselves, mull over it, and open our hearts to it during those times of silence in the church service.

103

Instead you thrill to GOD'S Word,
    you chew on Scripture day and night.

Ps. 1:2 MSG

Another way of using the church service as a form of meditation is to think back on the service itself to what was said in the sermon, to a hymn or song, to the reading or the Lord's supper. In Psalm 63, David reflects on his worship experience in the temple: "I have seen you in the sanctuary and beheld your power and your glory....On my bed I remember you; I think of you through the watches of the night" (Ps. 63:2, 6 NIV).

Psychologists have documented what has come to be called the negativity bias: in everyday life, "bad is stronger than good." It is not uncommon to have a day ruined by a single negative event. The neuropsychologist Rick Hanson captures this truth by telling us the brain seems designed to be "Velcro for bad experiences but Teflon for good ones." I can remember a dinner after church when I was in seminary, during which the initial conversation consisted of the host family mentioning the sermon bloopers, fashion faux pas, and other annoyances from church. I do not doubt the accuracy of what they reported, but I did notice how the good of worshiping God and hearing his Word had been drowned out by the bad. One of the simplest ways of meditating in church is simply to pause and savor the good. Perhaps after a hymn or a Scripture reading, you just take in what you heard and savor it as you would fine chocolate.

Seek to meditate on the Scripture that is read in the service. When the reading is finished, take a moment to gently repeat a verse or phrase you heard that struck you. The sermon and Lord's Supper provide an opportunity for one to take to heart the truth seen, heard, and tasted.

When you open your
Bible, lay down your need
to be strong, smart, and
independent. Pray with
the Psalmist, "Make me
understand the way of your
precepts, and I will meditate
on your wondrous works."
(Psalm 119:27)

Marshall Segal

I still remember a testimony of God's faithfulness I heard in college over fifty years ago. It was given by a physicist who was at the top of his game academically. He said that as a graduate student, he was facing great doubts. As he thought about casting aside his faith, he was comforted by Peter's observation, made when Jesus noted that many of his followers were leaving. Jesus asked the Twelve if they were going to leave him also. Peter responded, "Lord, to whom shall we go? You have the words of eternal life" (John 6:68 NIV). I am certain that in dozens of times of doubt or discouragement, I have used this verse as a comfort. This is what the psalmist described when he said, "One generation commends your works to another... and I will meditate on your wonderful works" (Ps. 145:4-5 NIV). I have meditated on the testimony of that faithful physicist. And words of testimony in the worship service provide an easy way to encourage people to meditate on God's "wonderful works."

### Meditation Groups

A decade ago, I was at a retreat focused on learning patterns of Christian meditation. In an opening meeting, the speaker asked how many of the attendees had learned to meditate on their own, and only one or two hands went up in the audience of one hundred. Biblical meditation is something that we oftentimes learn best in groups, and then we are able to practice on our own. Retreats and group settings offer us the space to have uninterrupted time to meditate. Whenever we learn a new skill, whether it be a sport or a musical instrument, there is an initial beginner's awkwardness that makes it hard to continue. When you have signed up and driven some distance to go

First, we are to meditate throughout life upon an everlasting Sabbath rest from all our works, that the Lord may work in us through his Spirit. Secondly, each one of us privately, whenever he has leisure, is to exercise himself diligently in pious meditation upon God's works.

John Calvin

on a retreat, you find that you have been given the space to do what you want to in ordinary life but that it is made easier in a retreat atmosphere. During one semester, I was able to go to a series of meditation classes, and I benefited immensely from knowing that there was an hour set aside for me to enter into that space and engage in the process. I have also benefited immensely from being in a small group of men that meditate weekly on Scripture. The time set aside and the support of others helps deepen my practice. With many things, when we are seeking to learn a new skill, we join a class or a club, and the camaraderie and support of others helps us. The Chicago Marathon is in October, so in early fall I see groups of runners heading out, and I meet groups of runners on their long runs as I am out running. I know the benefit of running groups; I returned to running in middle age and I do not think I would have continued without the support of my running group. The same is true for meditation groups. Not only do they spur you on, but they also help you learn techniques and strategies. You are encouraged, and you hear about the struggles and testimonies of those who have persevered. Find a Christian meditation group in a church and join it.

Spontaneous meditation throughout the day and meditation in your church service are the meditative practices most often portrayed in the Bible. These practices, which take no time but fill your time, can provide the foundation for dwelling in the Word. In the next chapter, we will look at formal meditation, which many people find provides the grounding for a life of spontaneous meditation on Scripture.

# – 8 –

# Sitting Alone with the Word of God

> To be alone with the Holy Scriptures! I dare not! When I turn up a passage in it, whatever comes to hand—it catches me instantly, it questions me (indeed it is as if it were God Himself that questioned me), "Hast thou done what thou readest there?" And then, then...yes, then I am caught. So then it is action at once, or instantly a humiliating admission.
>
> Oh, to be alone with the Holy Scriptures!—and if thou art not, then thou art not reading the Holy Scriptures.
>
> Søren Kierkegaard

Formal meditation is when you have set aside time to meditate on Scripture. This is a helpful practice, but I believe that one can fulfill the call of Psalm 1 and Joshua 8 to meditate and prosper simply through spontaneous meditation and by meditation arising from worship services. Many of us, particularly Christian leaders, have found that deliberate meditation on Scripture enriches our spontaneous meditation and is a necessary practice for us to stay grounded in God's presence.

Very early in the morning,
while it was still dark, Jesus
got up, left the house and
went off to a solitary place,
where he prayed.

Mark 1:35 NIV

# GWLW: God's Word the Last Word

This one of the most simple patterns of formal meditation. "God's Word the Last Word" (GWLW) means that you find a way to make your last thought before you fall asleep to be the Bible or a biblical theme or promise. Jim Downing suggests, "We need to give God the night key to our hearts. That night key is the Word of God." I had heard about this practice when I was in college. I thought it was a good idea, but I dismissed it at the time. And years later, I stumbled upon this concept again; a friend who struggled mightily with negative thinking mentioned how valuable this practice had been for him. Partly out of a desire to share his enthusiasm and be in solidarity with him, I decided to try it, and soon I realized its power in settling my mind. For some time, I selected a verse in the morning that I would use for GWLW, but now as I go to bed, I simply think about a verse that I have prayed in the evening prayer, or very often, I review the Ten Commandments or another verse of Scripture.

There has been a long practice in the Christian church of praying the compline prayer. The name compline comes from a Latin word indicating the completion of the day. This would have been the final prayer for those in religious orders who were praying seven times throughout the day. I use the liturgy in the Book of Common Prayer. There is wisdom in ending your day with Scripture. The compline liturgy is filled with Scripture and gives you phrases you can use for GWLW as you fall asleep. Praying this way helps to center you on God's grace, love, and trust.

When people tell me they
don't know how to meditate,
I reassure them by asking,
"Can you worry?" If they
know how to worry, they
know how to meditate.

Jan Johnson

## Bible Reading Meditation

The daily practice of reading the Bible is a long-established Christian practice. There are a myriad of Bible reading programs that suggest a text for each day. Bible reading and meditation go hand in hand, but they are not the same. In Bible reading, you seek breadth of exposure; in meditation, you go slowly and deeply.

You can either pause to meditate as you read or go back and ponder a passage after you finish your reading. To help develop a pattern of meditation that works well, you may want to limit the amount you are reading at first. Perhaps read short passages, or stay with a rich passage such as Psalm 23 or Galatians 5 for an entire month. The Book of Psalms is an excellent place to begin biblical meditation. The Psalms have long been the go-to place for Christian meditation. They require imagination to see and unpack the images. Using your God-given imagination is critical to the openhearted reading foundational to meditation.

The process of meditation is quite simple. Through prayer, remember that you are in God's presence and invite him to show you what is essential for you to see. Read the passage through and come to a settled sense of what the passage is about. You may find it helpful to use a study Bible to remind you of the context and to answer questions you have about words or images. Next, read the passage out loud. I cannot emphasize enough the importance of vocalizing your reading and writing down the portions you are drawn to. Again, the Hebrew words for meditation denote active engagement through speaking, singing, or muttering. After you have read the passage out loud a few times,

...just as you do not analyze the words of someone you love, but accept them as they are said to you, accept the Word of Scripture and ponder it in your heart... That is all. That is meditation.

Dietrich Bonhoeffer

settle on a portion that has caught your attention. You focus on this selection by seeking to savor it, taking it into your heart, and asking personal questions about it. Tim Keller writes, "Meditation consists in large part of asking the right questions." The process of questioning should be gentle, done with curiosity, and with a quest to learn from God about God and yourself.

Pray, sit in God's presence, read out loud, gently ask questions, write notes, and end with prayer. It is as simple as that, and it will change your life.

## Meditating Using Structured Questions

In this section, I am describing a process of planned meditation on the Bible. This is what many people think of when they hear the term biblical meditation. I have sought to make clear that this is one way to meditate, but it is not the only way, and the process I describe would not have been possible before the advent of printed books and readily available writing supplies. Before I describe the method I use, I provide some suggestions on how to set up your time of meditation.

I have found it valuable to set a timer to bound my meditation. When the timer is set, I can just give the time to meeting with God through the Bible. I do not have to be concerned that I will lose track of time and miss an appointment, and the bracketed time helps me guard against distractions. We are embodied beings, and physical cues help me enter into my time with God. Sitting in the same chair and using the same Bible and notebook can all help put one in a meditative frame of mind. Here are a few other suggestions for how to start your practice.

However, love chiefly trains us in meditation. Luther remarks: "Wherever love goes, there the heart and the body follow...Love itself will teach meditation...It is the mode and nature of all who love, to chatter, sing, think, compose, and frolic freely about what they love and enjoy hearing about it."

John Kleinig

We live in a future-oriented world of planning and doing, but to meet God, we need to be in the present moment. Two everyday activities that bring us into the present are savoring food and making or attentively listening to music. I begin my times of morning meditation by savoring a cup of tea. Enjoying the complex flavors of the tea helps bring me into the present moment. Many people find that singing a simple worship song brings them out of the future and into the moment.

Take a few minutes to "calm and quiet" yourself. The tried-and-true way to do this is to take a few minutes (consider using a timer) to simply watch one's breath. Why the breath? This has been a practice that Christians have suggested for at least 1,500 years. It is a way of grounding us in the present moment, and there is a clear analogy from breath to spirit. In Hebrew and Greek, the word for "breath" is also used for "spirit." When we watch our breath, we are subtly reminded of the reality of the presence of the Holy Spirit.

You may want to do a simple grounding activity to help you fully arrive at the meditation time. You could take a moment to light a candle as a reminder that this is time set aside and that God is present. Observe the flame and pray a prayer inviting God to be present. If you find yourself scattered, use your senses to help ground you. Perhaps grab tightly onto your chair and notice the sensations, or begin your meditation while walking slowly. Use the first minute to observe your steps, and when your mind wanders during the meditation, direct your attention to walking.

We practice biblical meditation to meet with God and enjoy the pleasure of his company. We also know

Oh Book! Infinite sweetness! let my heart
    Suck ev'ry letter, and a honey gain,
    Precious for any grief in any part;
To clear the breast, to mollify all pain.

George Herbert

that we will be changed through meditation: "Such a one is like a tree planted near streams; it bears fruit in season and its leaves never wither, and every project succeeds" (Ps. 1:3 NJB). One of the results of meditation is that we will produce fruit. We will be a more positive presence in our families, communities, and places of work. Because Christian meditation is done for the benefit of others, I think it is helpful to think of those in your social circle who will benefit when you bear more fruit. You may want to say, "Lord, I dedicate my time to _____, who will benefit from my growing in love and gentleness."

Here I share a simple way I have found helpful to undertake prayerful meditation. I set aside one page in a notebook. I date the page at the top, and then I draw a couple of lines on the page to set it up.

I draw a line down the right margin about an inch from the edge, and at the top of this column, I write "to do." This is where I write down those distracting thoughts that come to mind. I learned this practice from a pastor forty years ago, and it has been a simple practice that has enabled me to quiet my mind and given me focus. I realized early on in meditation that if I did not write down the need to pick up milk on the way home or to call a colleague, I would find that remembering the milk and calling Fred would become the subtext of my meditation. I write down those things that come to mind, and then I do not need to focus on them.

Across the bottom of the page, about an inch from the bottom, I draw another line. I write an L and circle it to set it apart. The L stands for listening; this is where I write down things that may have impressed me as I read and meditated on the passage. I may have

The Scriptures are designed to appeal to our faithful imagination...[I]n almost every verse of the Bible we have imagery: pictures of God, of ourselves, and of the world around us. That's why meditation is so important for our reception of God's Word. When we meditate, we use our imagination faithfully, as enlightened by the Holy Spirit, to see what God is saying to us in a particular passage.

John Kleinig

been impressed with the need to care for the poor, or perhaps I saw the tenderness of God's love more deeply. I will jot it down in a few words. These notes are helpful when I go back every month and read through this notebook to see what I noted and what phrases came to mind in the rest of the journal. It is also important to be open every time you sit for formal meditation with an awareness of God's presence with you to listen for a sense of what God is impressing on you. Without any sense of presumption or demand, we meditate expecting to hear from God and agree to linger until we do.

I then read a short passage out loud a few times and pause to think about its meaning. I write a brief answer to the question: What is the main point of this passage? This is not the time or place to take the time to do a prolonged study of the passage. You may find the notes in a study Bible helpful in understanding the context. This is important because it helps ground your meditation in the text. You are going to meditate on the text, not the big idea of the passage, but taking time to write out your sense of what the passage is about helps ground your meditation.

I then write out the passage or the portion I want to focus on. I write it out at the top of the page. Reading out loud and writing out the passage respects the physical nature of meditation in the Old Testament. In Deuteronomy, when a new king came to the throne, he was to write out a copy of the law and to read it for the rest of his life. This passage suggests the importance of writing out Scripture as a way of getting it into one's heart. "When he takes the throne of his kingdom, he is to write for himself on a scroll a copy of this law, taken from that of the

We live, in fact, in a world
starved for solitude, silence,
and privacy, and therefore
starved for meditation and
true friendship.

C. S. Lewis

Levitical priests. It is to be with him, and he is to read it all the days of his life so that he may learn to revere the LORD his God and follow carefully all the words of this law and these decrees" (Deut. 17:18–19 NIV).

Good meditation often flows from simple questions one asks of the text. I ask five questions that were shaped by a delightful book by Martin Luther. It is a letter he wrote to his barber, answering the barber's question about how to pray. He begins the letter this way: "I will tell you as best I can what I do personally when I pray." Luther tells his barber with pastoral tenderness and remarkable candor how he prays and meditates. He tells of "fashioning a garland of four entwined strands." as he meditates on Scripture. The four strands (see list below), influenced by Tim Keller's summary, are as follows (using the acronym TACTS):

- Teaching (T): What is the main point of this passage? What does it say about God and what he has done?

- Adoration (A): What does this call me to praise God for? Pray this truth back to God.

- Confession (C): How do I fail to live this out? Confess your failure back to God.

- Gospel Thanks & Aspiration (T): How do I see Christ as the best picture of this truth? How can this passage, with Christ's help, flourish in my life?

- Supplication (S): What does this passage call me to pray for?

I write down the four titles—T, A, C, T, S—and give a brief response to each question. This is not the

Some need or urgency in me "mines" all experience to find what is useful for my condition. This is the root of all meditation—name it as we will.

Howard Thurman

time for long and thoughtful answers. A phrase or a single word is sufficient to serve as guidance for your meditation. Your responses will often be brief and sketchy, but they need to be long enough to prompt you to be exact in your thinking. With this initial spade work done on the passage, you can begin to gently repeat the passage out loud and offer your prayers, confessions, and praises to God. What I found so helpful in Luther's guidance was a way of keeping both the biblical text and the presence of God in focus during my meditation.

## Meditating on Bible Stories

The Bible contains several types of writing, such as stories, poetry, and law, with stories being the most common genre. We love stories; they draw us in and capture and hold our attention. Years ago, a friend was preparing to fill in for his pastor at a meeting, and he asked his kindergarten son what he should teach. His son responded, "tell them a story." He knew intuitively that we are wired to appreciate stories.

When I talk with Christians who in the midst of making an important decision, I inevitably find that they turn to Bible stories for guidance. The experiences of Joseph, Esther, and Hannah have become more than ancient history for them and are part of their faith maps that guide them. Stories and especially the events in the gospels are given to provide us models and pictures of how to live. However, to benefit from these biblical stories we need to engage them with our imaginations as we read and meditate. That does not mean we enter a world of make-believe, but rather that we read and ponder the stories using our imaginations

Oh, how I love your law!
I meditate on it all day long.

Ps. 119:97 NIV

(our image-making and image-perceiving capacity). As we ask questions about the details of the story, the sparse and unembellished stories of the Bible come to life.

Consider the story of Jesus's forgiving and healing the paralytic in Mark 2. This brief story is packed with actions: a house jammed with people, Jesus teaching, a man being lowered through the roof by friends, controversy with religious leaders, Jesus pronouncing forgiveness and then healing the man. To engage the story thoughtfully, you need to use your imagination to see his friends digging a hole in the hard mud roof while Jesus and all the people look up in surprise. A study Bible can help you understand the setting. Read slowly and seek to picture with your mind's eye what is being described. Identify the universal human experience in the story (supportive friendship, creative problem-solving, and anger when beliefs are challenged) and reflect on how your own experience lines up with what is portrayed. Stories are designed to engage your imagination, so take the time to appreciate the rich artistic presentation of both human experience and God at work.

Often, reading and meditating are pretty ordinary. They are like the everyday moments in a long-term friendship or marriage that form the seedbed for those moments of sharing and care.

# − 9 −

# In Conclusion

We are to hear. All of us are. That is
what the whole Bible is calling out...
But hear what? The Bible is hundreds
upon hundreds of voices all calling at
once out of the past and clamoring for
our attention like barkers at a fair, like
air-raid sirens...Some of the voices are
shouting, like Moses' voice, so all Israel,
all the world, can hear, and some are
so soft and halting that you can hardly
hear them at all, like Job with ashes
on his head and his heart broken...
And somewhere in the midst of them all
one particular voice speaks out that is
unlike any other voice because it speaks
so directly to the deepest privacy and
longing and weariness of each of us
that there are times when the centuries
are blown away like mist, and it is as if
we stand with no shelter of time at all
between ourselves and the one who
speaks our secret name. Come, the voice
says. Unto me. All ye. Every last one.

Frederick Buechner

Meditation on Scripture is done in the presence
of God and as a way to open ourselves to his work in
our lives. This is well illustrated in Psalm 119. This
psalm celebrates Scripture's beauty and wisdom and

...through faithful meditation on the Word and by virtue of our union with Christ in the Spirit. God is present to us through the biblical Word as the living Christ speaks to us by his Spirit.

John Jefferson Davis

describes the joy of meditation. The psalmist fills the psalm with pleas to God for assistance in rightly engaging Scripture. More than fifty times, he calls out with cries such as, "open my eyes," "teach me," "give me understanding," "incline my heart," and "make your face shine." Meditation in Psalm 119 is not a skill one possesses but part of a relationship marked by love, respect, and deeply acknowledged need. Meditation, then, should involve a constant dialog with God about what is the subject of meditation.

All Christian meditation is done with an awareness of God with us—it is "thinking in the presence of God." Prayer and meditation are spiritual siblings. They are not the same, but they are closely related. As you meditate with the Bible, prayer comes as naturally as your next breath, and then you shift your focus back to poring over the text. Then you notice your heart warming with a deeply felt sense of God's presence or the underscoring of the reality of what you are muttering over and over. Pause and savor those moments of validation. We should treasure these, but we must not seek to replicate them. C. S. Lewis rightly warns, "It would be rash to say that there is any prayer which God never grants. But the strongest candidate is the prayer we might express in the single word 'encore'." Meditation is one way we open our hearts to experience God's love and grace and allow the divine physician to heal our hearts as well.

Who would want to complain about healing a blind man—a man blind since birth? Yet the fact that Jesus healed this blind man on the Sabbath did not sit well with the religious leaders, who thought Jesus' miracles were getting him far too much positive attention. The religious leaders went after

Meditation and study differ. Study is a work of the brain, meditation of the heart; study sets the invention on work, meditation sets the affection on work. Study is the finding out of a truth, meditation is the spiritual improvement of a truth; the one searcheth for the vein of gold, the other digs out the gold. Study is like a winter sun that hath little warmth and influence: meditation leaves one in a holy frame: it melts the heart when it is frozen, and makes it drop into tears of love.

Thomas Watson
(Watson and Smith 1995, 106)

the healed man and hunted down his parents. When the man spoke in defense of Jesus, they challenged him, saying, " 'You're nothing but dirt! How dare you take that tone with us!' Then they threw him out in the street" (John 9:34 MSG). After this story is told, in John's Gospel, Jesus gave an extended teaching in which he set himself in contrast to these teachers. He said that he is the good shepherd who "came that they may have life, and have it abundantly" (John 10:10 NRSV). Remember the promise of Psalm 1 for those who meditate? "They are like trees planted along the riverbank, bearing fruit each season. Their leaves never wither, and they prosper in all they do" (Ps. 1:3 NLT). Jesus desires that we put down our roots in the spiritual soil of God's love, and one way we do this is by meditating on God's truth and beauty in his Word. God gives this remarkable promise, and human flourishing in Christ is tied to this simple practice.

# Old Testament Allusions in Mary's Magnificat

In December 2022, Peter J. Williams of Tyndale House (Cambridge, UK) presented a Christmas devotion to an online audience. He focused on the way that Mary's Song was saturated with Old Testament references. I drew heavily from Peter's work when I created this table, which shows the many connections between the Old Testament and Mary's Song.

In this table, the first column shows the verses from Luke 1, the second column has the portion of the Mary's Song and the third column contains the Old Testament allusion or quotation. In this table all Bible quotations are from the NIV, unless otherwise specified.

| 46–47 | My soul glorifies the Lord and my spirit rejoices in God my Savior | Ps. 34:2–3 My soul makes its boast in the LORD; let the humble hear and be glad. Oh, magnify the LORD with me (ESV) Ps. 66:16 Come and hear, all you who fear God; let me tell you what he has done for me. Ps. 69:30 I will praise God's name in song and glorify him with thanksgiving. Ps. 35:9 Then my soul will rejoice in the LORD and delight in his salvation. |

| 48 | for he has been mindful of the humble state of his servant. From now on all generations will call me blessed | Ps. 71:17 Let his name be blessed through the ages; his name shall endure longer than the sun. And all the tribes of the earth will be blessed in him; all the nations will pronounce him happy. (NETS) Ps. 30:8 I will rejoice and be glad in your mercy, because you looked upon my humiliation; you saved my soul from dire straits (NETS) Ps. 34:2 My soul will make its boast in the LORD; The humble will hear it and rejoice. (NASB) |
|---|---|---|
| 49 | for the Mighty One has done great things for me—holy is his name. | Ps. 126:3 The LORD has done great things for us, and we are filled with joy. Ps. 71:19 Your righteousness, God, reaches to the heavens, you who have done great things. Who is like you, God? Ps. 126:2 Our mouths were filled with laughter, our tongues with songs of joy... "The LORD has done great things for them." |

| 50 | His mercy extends to those who fear him, from generation to generation. | Deut. 5:10 ...but showing love to a thousand generations of those who love me and keep my commandments.<br>Ps. 89:1 I will sing of the LORD'S great love forever; with my mouth I will make your faithfulness known through all generations.<br>Ps. 100:5 For the LORD is good and his love endures forever; his faithfulness continues through all generations. |
|---|---|---|
| 51–52 | He has performed mighty deeds with his arm; he has scattered those who are proud in their inmost thoughts. He has brought down rulers from their thrones but has lifted up the humble. | Ps. 89:10 You crushed Rahab like one of the slain; with your strong arm you scattered your enemies.<br>Ps. 147:6 The LORD sustains the humble but casts the wicked to the ground.<br>Ps 75:7 It is God who judges: He brings one down, he exalts another.<br>Job 5:11 The lowly he sets on high, and those who mourn are lifted to safety. |
| 53 | He has filled the hungry with good things but has sent the rich away empty. | Ps. 34:10 The lions may grow weak and hungry, but those who seek the LORD lack no good thing.<br>Ps. 107:9 for he satisfies the thirsty and fills the hungry with good things. |

| 54-55 | He has helped his servant Israel, remembering to be merciful to Abraham and his descendants forever, just as he promised our ancestors. | Ps. 98:3 He has remembered his love and his faithfulness to Israel; all the ends of the earth have seen the salvation of our God. Is. 41:8 But you, Israel, my servant, Jacob, whom I have chosen, you descendants of Abraham my friend Mic. 7:20 You will be faithful to Jacob, and show love to Abraham, as you pledged on oath to our ancestors in days long ago. |

# For Further Reading

Allcock, Linda. 2020. *Deeper Still: Finding Clear Minds and Full Hearts through Biblical Meditation.* Epsom, UK: The Good Book Company.

Clear and simple presentation with engaging personal reflections

Balthasar, Hans Urs von. 1989. *Christian Meditation.* San Francisco: Ignatius Press.

A brief Catholic contemplative exploration of Christian meditation

Bonhoeffer, Dietrich. 1986. *Meditating on the Word.* 2 ed.: Cowley Publications.

A compilation of Bonhoeffer's writings on meditation

Downing, Jim. 1977. *Meditation: The Bible Tells You How.* Colorado Springs, CO: Navpress.

A brief and very concrete introduction to meditating on Scripture

Johnson, Jan. 2016. *Meeting God in Scripture: A Hands-on Guide to Lectio Divina.* Downers Grove, IL: IVP.

Clear guide with exercises to meditating and praying Scripture

Keller, Timothy. 2015. *The Songs of Jesus: A Year of Daily Devotions in the Psalms.* New York, NY: Viking.

A devotional guide that indirectly teaches one how to meditate on the Psalms

Kleinig, John W. 2008. *Grace upon Grace: Spirituality for today.* St. Louis, MO: Concordia Pub. House.

Contains an unusually rich and thoughtful chapter on biblical meditation

Kraegel, Irene. 2020. *The Mindful Christian: Cultivating a Life of Intentionality, Openness, and Faith.* Minneapolis, MN: Fortress Press.

Primarily focuses on mindfulness meditation which can be a useful starting place for biblical meditation

Mulholland, Robert. 2001. *Shaped by the Word: The Power of Scripture in Spiritual Formation.* Revised ed.: Upper Room.

A modern classic on the devotional use of Scripture.

Saxton, David W. 2015. *God's Battle Plan for the Mind: the Puritan Practice of Biblical Meditation.* Grand Rapids, Michigan: Reformation Heritage Books.

Provides an overview of Puritan writings on meditation

Watson, Thomas, and Hamilton Smith. 1995. *Gleanings from Thomas Watson: Extracts from the Writings.* Morgan, PA: Soli Deo Gloria.

Watson is one of the clearest Puritan writers on meditation

Wilhoit, James, and Evan B. Howard. 2012. *Discovering Lectio Divina: Bringing Scripture into Ordinary Life.* Downers Grove, IL: IVP.

Brief introduction to the ancient practice of lectio divina, a four-fold practice of meditation and praying scripture

# References

## Preface

Page iii    "Do not let me go into my work believing": John Baillie, *A Diary of Private Prayer*, Updated and revised. ed. (New York: Scribner, 2014), 47.

## Chapter 1: The Way of Flourishing

Page 1    "Blessed Lord, who caused all holy Scriptures to be written for our learning": Episcopal Church, *The Book of Common Prayer* (New York: Seabury Press, 1979), 236.

Page 2    "Now there is in the Holy Scriptures a book": Dietrich Bonhoeffer, *Psalms: The Prayer Book of the Bible* (Augsburg Fortress, 1974), 13, 15.

Page 3    "I love the prairie!": Marilynne Robinson, *Gilead* (New York: Farrar, Straus and Giroux, 2004), 246.

Page 4    Psalm 1 "Happy is the one": Nancy L. DeClaissé-Walford, Rolf A. Jacobson, and Beth LaNeel Tanner, *The Book of Psalms*, NICOT (Grand Rapids, MI: Eerdmans, 2014), 59.

Page 5    "By happiness I mean, not a slight": John Wesley, and Albert Outler, *The Works of John Wesley*, vol. 4, The Bicentennial Edition of the Works of John Wesley (Nashville, TN: Abingdon Press, 1984), 386.

Page 6     "The Psalms are the prayer book of the Bible": Timothy Keller, *Prayer: Experiencing Awe and Intimacy with God* (New York: Dutton, Penguin, 2014), 146.

Page 7     "But in the law . . . is his longing delight": Zoltán Haraszti, ed., *The Bay Psalm Book: A Facsimile Reprint of the First Edition of 1640* (Chicago: University of Chicago Press, 1956), A.

Page 8     "It is a good thing to let prayer": Martin Luther, Mary Jane Haemig, and Eric Lund, *Little Prayer Book, 1522 and a Simple Way to Pray, 1535: The Annotated Luther Study Edition* (Minneapolis: Fortress Press, 2017), 82.

Page 9     Report from Lifeway Research: Eric Geiger, Michael Kelley, and Philip Nation, *Transformational Discipleship: How People Really Grow* (Nashville, TN: B & H, 2012).

Page 9     "Bible engagement has an impact...spiritual growth": Lifeway Research, "Bible Engagement in Churchgoers' Hearts, Not Always Practiced - Lifeway Research," last modified 2012-09-06, 2012, https://research.lifeway.com/2012/09/06/bible-engagement-in-churchgoers-hearts-not-always-practiced/.

Page 9     "Best-practice churches make Bible engagement": Greg Hawkins, and Cally Parkinson, *Move: What 1,000 Churches Reveal About Spiritual Growth* (Grand Rapids, MI: Zondervan, 2011), 221, 225.

Page 10    "Without meditation the truths which we know will never affect our hearts": Thomas Watson, and Hamilton Smith, *Gleanings from Thomas Watson: Extracts from the Writings* (Morgan, PA: Soli Deo Gloria, 1995), 106, 112.

Page 12    "What each man worships": Origen, and Elizabeth Ann Dively Lauro, *Homilies on Judges, The Fathers of the Church*, vol. 119 (Washington, D.C.: Catholic University of America Press, 2010), 55.

## Chapter 2: True Spiritual Food

Page 15    "The light burns long in his study.": Rainer Maria Rilke, and Burton Pike, *The Notebooks of Malte Laurids Brigge*, 1st Dalkey Archive ed. (Champaign, IL: Dalkey Archive Press, 2008), 176.

Page 17    "In yourself, you rouse us": Augustine, *Confessions*, trans. Sarah Rudin (New York, NY: The Modern Library, 2017), 3.

Page 17    "For Augustine, the goal of life is knowing and enjoying God": Ellen T. Charry, *By the Renewing of Your Minds: The Pastoral Function of Christian Doctrine* (New York: Oxford, 1999), 128.

Page 18    "If I have time and opportunity": Martin Luther, Mary Jane Haemig, and Eric Lund, *Little Prayer Book, 1522 and a Simple Way to Pray, 1535: The Annotated Luther Study Edition* (Minneapolis: Fortress Press, 2017), 96.

Page 20    "Why do I meditate?": Dietrich Bonhoeffer, *Meditating on the Word*, 2 ed. (Cowley Publications, 1986), 30.

Page 21    Psalm 1: Nancy L. DeClaissé-Walford, Rolf A. Jacobson, and Beth LaNeel Tanner, *The Book of Psalms*, NICOT (Grand Rapids, MI: Eerdmans, 2014), 59.

Page 22    "Meditation, then, is what gives you stability": Timothy Keller, *Prayer: Experiencing Awe and Intimacy with God* (New York: Dutton, Penguin, 2014), 146-47

## Chapter 3: What is Meditation?

Page 27    "These are only a few suggestions": Macrina Wiederkehr, *Abide: Keeping Vigil with the Word of God* (Collegeville, MN: Liturgical Press, 2011), 6.

Page 28    "The word meditate as used in the Old Testament": Jerry Bridges, *The Practice of Godliness* (Colorado Springs, CO: Navpress, 1996), 44.

Page 29    meditate, v.: "meditate, v.". *OED Online*. December 2022. Oxford University Press. https://www.oed.com (accessed January 30, 2023).

Page 29    Coverdale Bible Translation: Myles Coverdale, The Coverdale Bible, 1535 (Folkestone, UK: Dawson, 1975).

Page 29    "to employ, bring to bear": "exercise, v." *OED Online*. December 2022. Oxford University Press. https://www.oed.com (accessed January 30, 2023).

Page 29    "They used many terms": John W. Kleinig, "The Attentive Heart: Meditation in the Old Testament," *The Reformed Theological Review* 51, no. 2 (1992): 51.

Page 30    "Meditation then is the deliberate appropriation": John W. Kleinig, "The Indwelling Word: Meditation in the New Testament," *The Reformed Theological Review* 51, no. 3 (1992): 83.

Page 30    "Like all spiritual disciplines": Jan Johnson, *Meeting God in Scripture: A Hands-on Guide to Lectio Divina* (Downers Grove, IL: IVP, 2016), 20.

Page 30    "Meditation is the activity of calling to mind": J. I. Packer, *Knowing God* (Downers Grove, IL: IVP, 1973), 18-19.

Page 30    "Christian meditation, very simply": Richard J. Foster, *Celebration of Discipline: The Path to Spiritual Growth*, 3rd ed. (San Francisco: HarperSanFrancisco, 1998), 17.

Page 30    "let's define meditation as deep thinking": Donald S. Whitney, *Spiritual Disciplines for the Christian Life*, Revised and Updated ed. (Colorado Springs, CO: NavPress, 2014, 2014), 46-47.

Page 32    "Pray over your meditations": Thomas Watson, and Hamilton Smith, *Gleanings from Thomas Watson: Extracts from the Writing*s (Morgan, PA: Soli Deo Gloria, 1995), 113.

Page 33    "whole mind with all its faculties": John W. Kleinig, *Grace Upon Grace: Spirituality for Today* (St. Louis, MO: Concordia, 2008), 87.

Page 33    "The decisive thing is not how we meditate":
           John W. Kleinig, "Meditation," Logia 10, no. 2
           (Eastertide 2001): 46.

Page 34    "On some days, stand as a pilgrim before the
           Word of God.": Macrina Wiederkehr, *Abide:
           Keeping Vigil with the Word of God* (Collegeville,
           MN: Liturgical Press, 2011), 8.

Page 36    "Let us mourn before the Lord": Edmund
           Calamy, *The Art of Divine Meditation* (London:
           Thomas Parkhurst—EBBO, 1719), 202-03.

Page 37    "Pray as you can, and do not try to pray as you
           can't": John Chapman, *The Spiritual Letters of
           Dom John Chapman, O.S.B.* (London: Sheed and
           Ward, 1935), 109.

## Chapter 4: Meditation and Jesus' Spiritual Formation

Page 37    "When we meditate on a saying or scene of
           the Gospel": Hans Urs von Balthasar, *Christian
           Meditation* (San Francisco: Ignatius Press, 1989),
           34.

Page 40    "Meditation is the intensification...of the
           Word.": Simon Chan, *Spiritual Theology: A
           Systematic Study of the Christian Life* (Downers
           Grove, IL: IVP, 1998), 166-67.

Page 42    "Simply meditate...on the life and mysteries
           of Jesus Christ": Jean-Pierre de Caussade,
           *Abandonment to Divine Providence* (St. Louis, MO:
           B. Herder Book Co., 1921), 361.

Page 43    "The mother that God chose for Jesus was immersed in the Scriptures": Peter J. Williams, Peter's Fireside Christmas Devotion, Tyndale House Newsletter (Cambridge (UK): 2022).

Page 44    "In his Gospel, Luke portrays Mary": Kleinig, *Grace Upon Grace: Spirituality for Today*, 116-17.

Page 46    "Through Scripture reading, we expose ourselves to the text": James Wilhoit, and Evan B. Howard, *Discovering Lectio Divina: Bringing Scripture into Ordinary Life* (Downers Grove, IL: IVP, 2012), 79.

Page 47    "Their amazement must relate": Jan Willem Doeve, "Jewish Hermeneutics in the Synoptic Gospels and Acts" (Thesis, Leiden, 1953), 105.

Page 48    "According to Psalm 1" Timothy Keller, *Prayer: Experiencing Awe and Intimacy with God* (New York: Dutton, Penguin, 2014), 146-47

Page 49    "The understanding with which his mind grasped": R. C. H. Lenski, *The Interpretation of St. Luke's Gospel* (Columbus,OH: Wartburg, 1946), 164-65.

Page 50    "in informational reading we seek to grasp the control": Robert Mulholland, *Shaped by the Word: The Power of Scripture in Spiritual Formation*, Revised ed. (Upper Room, 2001), 54, 57-58.

Page 51    Jesus' use of Old Testament: Robert P. Lightner, *The Saviour and the Scriptures* (Grand Rapids, MI: Baker, 1978), 28-29.

Page 51    Jesus' use of Old Testament: Steve Moyise, "Jesus
           and the Scriptures of Israel," in *Handbook for the
           Study of the Historical Jesus*, ed. Tom Holmén and
           Stanley Porter, vol. 2 (Boston: Brill, 2011), 122–
           23.

Page 51    "Yet he frequently offered interpretations of
           Scripture": Charles Kimball, *Jesus' Exposition of
           the Old Testament in Luke's Gospel, Journal for the
           Study of the New Testament*. Supplement Series,
           94 (Sheffield, UK: JSOT Press, 1994), 197.

Page 51    "Jesus lived in the Old Testament": Joachim
           Jeremias, New Testament Theology: The
           Proclamation of Jesus (London: S.C.M. Press,
           1971), 205–06.

Page 52    "Our anxieties and injuries": Kleinig, *Grace Upon
           Grace: Spirituality for Today*, 93.

Page 56    "There are not many rules":       Jean Calvin,
           *Institutes of the Christian Religion*, ed. John
           McNeil, trans. Ford Lewis Battles, The Library
           of Christian Classics, V. 20–21 (Philadelphia:
           Westminster, 1960), I:362.

Page 58    "As you move from reading to meditation":
           Kenneth Boa, *Conformed to His Image: Biblical and
           Practical Approaches to Spiritual Formation* (Grand
           Rapids, Mich.: Zondervan, 2001), 177.

Page 60    "In the timeless story of Mary and Martha":
           Irene Kraegel, *The Mindful Christian: Cultivating
           a Life of Intentionality, Openness, and Faith*
           (Minneapolis, MN: Fortress, 2020), 44.

## Chapter 5: Meditating on Scripture

Page 66     "Consider or think on": Bonnie Bowman Thurston, and Judith Ryan, *Philippians and Philemon*, vol. 10, Sacra Pagina (Collegeville, MN: Liturgical Press, 2005), 147.

Page 68     "Read the text, re-read it, re-read it and read it again": John R. W. Stott, *Between Two Worlds: The Challenge of Preaching Today* (Grand Rapids, MI: Eerdmans 2017), 170.

Page 70     "Meditation may be thus described": Thomas Watson, *Heaven Taken by Storm: Or, the Holy Violence a Christian Is to Put Forth in the Pursuit after Glory* (London: W. Justins, 1788), 35.

Page 73     "God's address is at-the-end-your-rope. com": Gary W. Moon, *Becoming Dallas Willard: The Formation of a Philosopher, Teacher, and Christ Follower* (Downers Grove, IL: IVP, 2018), 7.

Page 74     "Our "being still" as Christians": Pablo Martinez, Take Care of Yourself: Survive and Thrive in Christian Ministry (Peabody, MA: Hendrickson, 2018), 77.

Page 75     "Always we begin again": John McQuiston, *Always We Begin Again: The Benedictine Way of Living*, Revised edition ed. (New York: Morehouse Publishing, 2011).

150

## Chapter 6: Meditation: The Pathway of Life

Page 77   "Have you not realized that most of your unhappiness": Martyn Lloyd-Jones, *Spiritual Depression: Its Cause and Its Cure* (Grand Rapids, MI: Eerdmans 1965), 20-21.

Page 78   "Another common form of spontaneous meditation": John W. Kleinig, *Grace Upon Grace: Spirituality for Today* (St. Louis, MO: Concordia, 2008), 90-91.

Page 82   "Some people like to read so many chapters": C. H. Spurgeon, *The Metropolitan Tabernacle Pulpit*, vol. 27 (London: Passmore & Alabaster, 1882), 42.

Page 83   "It is impossible for man to drive out": George Dokos, *The Watchful Mind: Teachings on the Prayer of the Heart* (Yonkers, NY: St. Vladimir's, 2014), 42.

Page 84   "For the first period of my Christian life": Alister E. McGrath, *The Journey: A Pilgrim in the Lands of the Spirit*, 1st ed. (New York: Doubleday, 2000), 15-16.

Page 86   "To this day I suckle at the Lord's Prayer": Martin Luther, Mary Jane Haemig, and Eric Lund, *Little Prayer Book, 1522 and a Simple Way to Pray, 1535: The Annotated Luther Study Edition* (Minneapolis: Fortress Press, 2017), 96.

Page 88   "And there is nothing that so much strengthens our faith": Thomas Cranmer, "On Scripture," 1547, accessed August 25, 2022, http://archive.org/details/CranmerOnScripture.

## Chapter 7: Meditating in Everyday Life

Page 91    "There is a way of life so hid with Christ": Thomas R. Kelly, *A Testament of Devotion* (San Francisco: HarperSanFrancisco, 1996), 98.

Page 95    "This, then, is the devotional formula": John Cassian, *John Cassian: Conferences*, trans. Colm Luibheid, Classics of Western Spirituality (New York, NY: Paulist Press, 1985), 10.8.2.

Page 96    "a man may take into his understanding and memory": Richard Baxter, *The Saints' Everlasting Rest* (Fearn, Tain, UK: Christian Focus Publications, 1998), 549.

Page 100   "When I worked on translating": Bruce K. Waltke, *Finding the Will of God: A Pagan Notion?*, 2nd ed. (Grand Rapids, MI: Eerdmans, 2016), 92.

Page 101   "God's view of good fortune": Nancy L. DeClaissé-Walford, Rolf A. Jacobson, and Beth LaNeel Tanner, *The Book of Psalms*, NICOT (Grand Rapids, MI: Eerdmans, 2014), 387.

Page 101   "How, then, it may be asked, can we...avoid Him?: C. S. Lewis, "The Seeing Eye," in *Christian Reflections*, ed. Walter Hooper (Grand Rapids, MI: Eerdmans, 1967), 168.

Page 103   "The Divine Service is thus the school": John W. Kleinig, *Grace Upon Grace: Spirituality for Today* (St. Louis, MO: Concordia, 2008), 119.

Page 105    "bad is stronger than good": Roy F. Baumeister et al., "Bad Is Stronger Than Good," *Review of General Psychology* 5, no. 4 (2001).

Page 105    "Velcro for bad experiences but Teflon for good ones": Hanson Rick, *Hardwiring Happiness: The New Brain Science of Contentment, Calm and Confidence* (New York: Crown Publishing, 2013), 2.

Page 106    "When you open your Bible": Marshall Segal, "I Will Meditate on You in the Morning," desiringgod.org, 2018, accessed July 1, 2022, 2022, https://www.desiringgod.org/articles/i-will-meditate-on-you-in-the-morning.

Page 108    "First, we are to meditate": Jean Calvin, *Institutes of the Christian Religion*, ed. John McNeil, trans. Ford Lewis Battles, The Library of Christian Classics, V. 20-21 (Philadelphia: Westminster, 1960), I:400.

## Chapter 8: Sitting Alone with the Word of God

Page 111    "To be alone with the Holy Scriptures!": Søren Kierkegaard, *For Self-Examination and Judge for Yourself!*, trans. Walter Lowrie, Kierkegaard's Writings, vol. 21 (Princeton, NJ: Princeton, 1974), 56.

Page 113    "We need to give God the night key to our hearts.": Jim Downing, *Meditation: The Bible Tells You How* (Colorado Springs, CO: Navpress, 1977), 43.

Page 114    "When people tell me they don't know how to meditate": Jan Johnson, *When the Soul Listens: Finding Rest and Direction in Contemplative Prayer*, 2nd ed. (Colorado Springs, CO: NavPress, 2017), 55.

Page 116    "just as you do not analyze the words": Dietrich Bonhoeffer, and Edwin Hanton Robertson, *The Way to Freedom; 1935-1939, from the Collected Works of Dietrich Bonhoeffer, His Letters, Lectures and Notes*, V. 2 (New York: Harper & Row, 1966), 59.

Page 117    "Meditation consists in large part of asking the right questions": Timothy Keller, *The Songs of Jesus: A Year of Daily Devotions in the Psalms* (New York, NY: Viking, 2015), 180.

Page 118    "However, love chiefly trains us in meditation.": John W. Kleinig, *Grace Upon Grace: Spirituality for Today* (St. Louis, MO: Concordia, 2008), 94.

Page 120    "Oh Book! Infinite sweetness!": George Herbert, and Louis Lohr Martz, *George Herbert, The Oxford Poetry Library* (Oxford ; New York: Oxford University Press, 1994), 46.

Page 124    "We live, in fact, in a world starved for solitude, silence": C. S. Lewis, and Walter Hooper, *The Weight of Glory, and Other Addresses*, Rev. and expanded ed. (New York: Macmillan, 1980), 107.

Page 125    "I will tell you as best I can": Martin Luther, Mary Jane Haemig, and Eric Lund, *Little Prayer Book, 1522 and a Simple Way to Pray, 1535: The Annotated Luther Study Edition* (Minneapolis: Fortress Press, 2017), 82.

Page 125 "fashioning a garland of four entwined strands": Martin Luther, Mary Jane Haemig, and Eric Lund, *Little Prayer Book, 1522 and a Simple Way to Pray, 1535: The Annotated Luther Study Edition* (Minneapolis: Fortress Press, 2017), 96.

Page 125 Tim Keller's summary of Luther on Prayer: Timothy Keller, *Praying with the Psalms* (New York: Redeemer Presbyterian Church, 2008), 212.

Page 126 "Some need or urgency in me": Howard Thurman, *With Head and Heart: The Autobiography of Howard Thurman* (New York: Harcourt Brace Jovanovich, 1979), 263.

## Chapter 9: In Conclusion

Page 131 "We are to hear": Frederick Buechner, A Room Called Remember: Uncollected Pieces (San Francisco: Harper & Row, 1984), 37.

Page 132 "through faithful meditation on the Word": John Jefferson Davis, *Meditation and Communion: Contemplating Scripture in an Age of Distraction* (Downers Grove, IL: IVP Academic, 2012), 102.

Page 133 "thinking in the presence of God": Timothy Keller, *Prayer: Experiencing Awe and Intimacy with God* (New York: Dutton, Penguin, 2014), 92.

Page 133 "It would be rash to say that there is any prayer": C. S. Lewis, *Letters to Malcolm: Chiefly on Prayer* (New York: Harcourt, Brace & World, 1964), 27.

Page 134    "Meditation and study differ": Thomas Watson, and Hamilton Smith, *Gleanings from Thomas Watson: Extracts from the Writing*s (Morgan, PA: Soli Deo Gloria, 1995), 106.

Made in the USA
Monee, IL
28 May 2023

34806835R00089